Speaking Naturally

Communication Skills in American English

Bruce Tillitt
Mary Newton Bruder

CAMBRIDGE
UNIVERSITY PRESS

Published by the Press Syndicate of the University of Cambridge
The Pitt Building, Trumpington Street, Cambridge CB2 1RP
40 West 20th Street, New York, NY 10011-4211, USA
10 Stamford Road, Oakleigh, Melbourne 3166, Australia

First published 1985
Eighth printing 1995

Printed in the United States of America

Library of Congress Cataloging-in-Publication Data

Tillitt, Bruce.
Speaking naturally.
1. English language – Text-books for foreign speakers.
2. English language – United States – Spoken English.
3. Speech acts (Linguistics) I. Bruder, Mary Newton,
1939– . II. Title.
PE 1128.T54 1985 428.3′4. 84-5875

ISBN 0-521-27130-4 paperback
ISBN 0-521-25007-2 cassette

Book design by Peter Ducker
Illustrations by Jean Chandler
Cover design by Frederick Charles Ltd.
Cover illustration by Tom Ickert
Cassette production by The Sun Group

Contents

Acknowledgments

I would like to thank my wife, Patricia Carlson, for the original impetus from which this book came, and for her unwavering support of the writing thereof.

Bruce Tillitt

We are grateful to Patricia Furey, who has been very helpful in the shaping of the materials from the beginning. To the teachers and students in the advanced speaking classes at the English Language Institute, University of Pittsburgh, who have struggled with earlier versions of these materials and who have given us much valuable feedback go our heartfelt thanks.

We would also like to thank the following teachers especially: Peggy Allen for her "introductory quiz" technique, Peggy Anderson, Holly Deemer, Carol Jasnow, and Linda Schmandt.

Fran Williams and Dorothy H. Bruder deserve medals for the typing.

Bruce Tillitt
Mary Newton Bruder

To the teacher

Recent trends in ESL/EFL curriculum design and pedagogy have stressed the importance of teaching communicative strategies and the functional use of language. *Speaking Naturally* is designed to do just that: teach students how to perform certain language functions in English by presenting the social rules for language use.

Because native speakers acquire these rules as part of growing up, they do not need to make conscious reference to them as adults. Second language learners, however, need information about sociolinguistic rules that may differ from those in their own culture. We have found in the writing and testing of the materials that there is often disagreement about rules, depending on one's native region, sex, age, and so on. If you disagree with any of the sociolinguistic rules presented in the text or feel that they need modification, point this out to your students and discuss the differences.

Differences between informal and formal speech

In all languages the forms people use when speaking formally are different from those used informally. In English we tend to use formal speech with strangers and people of higher status, and informal speech with family, friends, and colleagues. Of course, language does not always fall into such neat categories as "formal" and "informal." The level of formality speakers choose depends upon their relationship, the setting, the topic being discussed, and many other factors. Students should be aware of the differences in speaking styles and the reasons for selecting the most appropriate style in a given situation.

Formal and informal speech are differentiated in this book in two basic ways: by style and by content. Informal speech is characterized stylistically by omissions, elisions, reductions, and, sometimes, a faster speaking rate. Formal speech is characterized by embedding (building information into sentences, also characteristic of written language) and a tendency toward more complete sentences as opposed to fragments. Consider, for instance, these examples of informal and formal language:

Informal	*Formal*
Sorry, gotta go.	I'm afraid I've got to be going now.
Wanna beer?	Could I offer you a beer?
He's a pain in the neck.	He has not been easy to deal with.

Formal and informal speech can also be differentiated on the basis of content. There are certain phrases appropriate in informal situations that are inappropriate in formal situations, such as "Got any change?" (which would not usually be asked of a stranger, for example).

Thus students need to know not only *how* to perform language functions but the cultural rules that determine *when* these functions are appropriate. Even classes at advanced levels may not have a great awareness of the different rules for speaking. In such a case you could ask questions concerning customs in the students' countries and discuss how these customs differ from those in North America, for example: When do you thank people? Is it acceptable to stop by someone's house without calling first? How would you get a waiter's attention in a restaurant?

As a warm-up activity, early in the semester, you might give the class a "quiz" like the following:

Which of the following are polite, rude, or neutral remarks?

You look thin.
You look like you've gained some weight.
How much does your apartment cost?
Can you lend me $5 until next week?
Do your parents fight a lot? (To a classmate.)
What a beautiful baby you have.
How much did your shoes cost?
Do you have any children? Why not?
What religion are you? (At a cocktail party.)
What grade did you get on your test? (To a fellow classmate.)
That color doesn't look good on you!

Introducing the unit

Each unit opens with one or two paragraphs that set the students' expectations for what is in each lesson. We recommend asking students to read this introduction silently before they listen to the dialogues. You could accompany this with a brief (5-minute) discussion of the topic in relation to the students' cultures.

1 DIALOGUES AND DISCUSSION

The dialogues are recorded on the Cassette (indicated by the symbol 📼). The students should listen to the recorded dialogues as they read along in the book. A discussion that focuses the students' attention on the teaching point (or recycles previous teaching points) follows each dialogue. A question about level of formality is presented each time, since this is the key to the language differences. The students should be asked to give evidence from the dialogues to support their answers.

2 READING

Students might read Section 2 in each unit for homework; you could review it briefly in the next class, answering questions and pointing out areas that diverge from the students' native cultures. If you do not know the students' cultures, it is often fun and instructive to be an amateur anthropologist and find out a few things about them. You could then spend some time discussing the differences between North American customs and those of other cultures.

3 PHRASES

The phrases are recorded on the Cassette (indicated by the symbol [▭]). Students should listen to the phrases on the tape as they read them in the book. You may want to have students repeat the phrases out loud. Point out grammar and pronunciation differences for different formality levels.

4 SMALL GROUP PRACTICE

The students work in pairs or small groups according to the directions for each exercise. If possible, group students with others from different language backgrounds to encourage them to use only English. Change the grouping frequently so that all the students get to know each other. No names have been used to designate the speakers, so the teacher can assign roles in the role plays and other exercises according to the class membership.

The groups practice simultaneously – the noise level gets pretty high at times – and then groups are selected to perform for the entire class. It would be boring for all the groups to perform each exercise, so you should avoid repeating the same exercise. However, there should be frequent "in front of class" performances with plenty of feedback from both you and students.

Feedback should be delayed until the end of the performance; the students should not be interrupted in mid-stream or they lose the thread of the conversation. Corrections should center on things that may interfere with communication, such as severe pronunciation problems or violations of the communicative competence rules. Feedback should also include comments on the appropriateness of language to the role. It is also a good idea to try to get the performers to correct their own errors if possible, with questions such as "Do you think a professor would really say _____?".

To the teacher

A. Using what you've learned

For classes of lower proficiency, these exercises can be assigned as homework before the performance in class. The students still need to practice in class, however.

B. Cued dialogues

These exercises allow the students to apply what they have learned without conducting a complete conversation from start to finish. The language functions are specified and the turns numbered, so that following the steps will create a fairly natural conversational exchange. A feedback discussion should follow.

C. Mini-roleplays

With these, the students have the most freedom to use what they have learned. Some expressions are suggested, but feel free to suggest others. The roleplays should be fairly short (3–5 minutes) and should be followed by a feedback discussion.

To the student

Speaking Naturally gives useful information about the kind of language that is appropriate in different situations. For example, how and when do you thank people? How do you invite your boss or professor to dinner? How do you invite a friend? What is the most polite way to interrupt? You already know the language and social rules for your own culture. How do they differ in America?

Throughout the units you will be asked to analyze the formality of the relationships between different people in the situations presented. We hope that when you finish you will be more comfortable using English in a variety of situations.

To help you listen for the differences, the dialogues at the beginning of each unit, and the phrases in Section 3 of each unit, are recorded on the Cassette (indicated by the symbol ⬛).

As you know, North America is made up of many different groups of people. Customs vary somewhat according to region and ethnic background, but generally the language is the same. If you have doubts about what to say in a particular situation, feel free to ask someone. Most Americans enjoy talking about their language.

1 Openings and closings

Opening a conversation and bringing a conversation to an end are essential parts of our everyday language. You already know how to say hello and good-bye, but in this lesson you will study in more detail how Americans perform these functions. You might notice some similarities, as well as some differences, if you compare American conversation openings and closings with those in your native culture.

In the dialogues that follow, listen carefully to what the speakers say to greet each other and what they say to indicate that the conversation is over. Notice especially how many interchanges it takes to end a conversation.

1 DIALOGUES 🔊

Dialogue A

Mike: Say, Grace, how you doing?*
Grace: Mike! Hey, how are you?
Mike: Not bad. Where you going?*
Grace: Over to Jerry's. How about you?
5 Mike: Oh, I just got off work. Boy, I'm so hungry I could eat a horse!
Grace: Where are you working now?
Mike: J & L Steel. It's a real pain. But I guess I shouldn't complain. Lots of guys are out of work these days.
10 Grace: Yeah, that's the truth. Well, I better let you go get some supper.*
Mike: Yeah. It was great seeing you again. Maybe we could get together sometime.
Grace: Sounds good.* I'll give you a call.
15 Mike: OK. Great. Well, I'll be seeing you.
Grace: OK, Mike. Enjoy your meal.
Mike: Thanks. Bye.
Grace: Bye.

get off work: finish working for the day
out of work: unemployed

Usage note: **How** (are) **you doing?**, **Where** (are) **you going?**, **I** (had) **better**, (It) **sounds good** are all examples of informal speech in which words are dropped.

Discussion

1. What do the two speakers call each other?
2. How do they greet each other? (What phrases do they use?)
3. What does Mike mean in line 8 when he says, "It's a real pain"?
4. How many exchanges does it take Mike and Grace to end their conversation?
5. How do Mike and Grace say good-bye? (What phrases do they use?)
6. Is this a formal conversation? How do you know?

Dialogue B

(*The telephone rings.*)

Dean Schubert: Hello. This is Virginia Schubert.

Fred Marshall: Hello, Dean Schubert. My name is Fred Marshall. I'm a reporter from the *Times*.

Dean Schubert: Yes?

5 Fred Marshall: I heard about a strange animal at your house. Could I come and talk to you about it?

Dean Schubert: Yes, it certainly would make an amusing story! Can you come this afternoon at three o'clock?

Fred Marshall: Yes, that would be fine. Thank you very much. I'll
10 see you then.

Dean Schubert: You're welcome. Good-bye.

Discussion

1. Why does Fred Marshall telephone Dean Schubert?
2. What words do they use to greet each other?
3. Why does Fred thank her?
4. What is the relationship of the speakers?
5. Is this dialogue more formal or less formal than Dialogue A?

Dialogue C

Jack: Oh, my gosh, that's Susie Johnson!

Mike: What?

Jack: Over by the bananas. Come on, let's go say hello. (*They go over to Susie.*) Hey, Susie!

5 Susie: What?... Jack?!

Jack: Hey, how are you? Gee, we haven't seen each other in... it must be close to three years!

Susie: Well, how have you been?

Jack: OK.

10 Susie: Still working at Lamstons?

Jack: Let's not go into that. Oh, Susie, this is Mike, one of my
   buddies at work.
Susie: Hi, Mike.
Mike: Hi, how are you?
15 Jack: Gee, we ought to go somewhere to talk. How about Peter's
   Pub?
Susie: Sounds good. Just give me a minute to pick up a few things
   for dinner tonight.
Jack: OK. See you at the check-out stand.

oh my gosh: an expression that shows surprise
gee: an expression that shows surprise (see Unit 6)
buddy: good friend
check-out stand: cashier; where you pay for what you buy

Discussion

1. How many people are there? Where are the speakers? What are
 they doing when this dialogue begins?
2. How does Jack say hello?
3. Identify the ages and relationships of the speakers.
4. What can you say about the level of formality here? Why is it
 appropriate?

2   GREETINGS, PRECLOSINGS, AND CLOSINGS

Greetings

Greetings in all languages have the same purpose: to establish contact with another person, to recognize his or her existence, and to show friendliness. The formulas for greeting are very specific and usually do not carry any literal meaning. People say "Good morning" even if it is a miserable day and may reply to "How are you?" with "Fine, thanks," even if they aren't feeling well.

The greeting is always returned, often in the same form but with different stress.

A: How *are* you?
B: Fine, thanks. How are *you*?

or

A: How are you?
B: Fine, thanks, and you?
A: Fine. (Thanks.)

People who are together every day greet one another the first time they meet each day. They do not shake hands.

When people have not seen each other for a long time, the greeting is often enthusiastic and is usually accompanied by shaking hands among men, hugging among both men and women, and sometimes a kiss on the cheek among women.

Preclosings and closings

Usually people do not suddenly quit talking, say good-bye, and leave each other abruptly; ending a conversation normally takes some time. This involves two kinds of interactions: preclosings and closings. *Preclosings* are phrases that signal the end of a conversation; *closings* are phrases that explicitly end the conversation.

There are some people with whom it is difficult to end a conversation. The problem is that they usually ignore the signals that end the conversation. With close friends this does not usually cause any severe difficulties; but with people we do not know well or with people in superior positions, it is considered rude to ignore preclosings. If someone ignores your first preclosing, you can use a stronger one (see Phrases section).

In formal situations, the superior (in age, status, etc.) usually signals the end of a conversation. On the telephone, the caller usually precloses. In informal situations, either speaker may preclose. Preclosings often include thanking a person for something (Unit 4) or making an excuse or apology (Unit 5).

Closings, like greetings, are commonly used exchanges with no literal meaning. People who are together every day say good-bye at the end of the day or week (and wish each other a nice weekend).

When leaving a party, guests always find the host or hostess to say thank you and good-bye. People who are leaving each other permanently or for a long time shake hands or embrace, depending on the relationship. If you are in an unfamiliar situation and wonder what to do, watch other people or ask.

Discussion

What gestures can you use for greeting someone in your country? Do you shake hands? If so, what are the rules for handshakes? How do you end a conversation in your country? Do you have certain expressions to show that you are ready for a conversation to end?

3 PHRASES 📼

Directions: Listen to the following phrases on the tape as you read along here. Then practice saying them. The phrases near the top of the list are generally more formal than the ones near the bottom.

	GREETINGS	RESPONSES
More formal	Good morning.	Good morning.
	Good afternoon.	Good afternoon.
	Good evening.	Good evening.
	How nice to see you!	Yes, it's been quite a while.
	What a pleasant surprise!	
	Hello, Robert.	Hello, Kathryn.
	How are you?	Fine, thanks. And you?
	Hi, Bob.	Hi, Kathy.
	How've you been?	Pretty good.
	What's happening?	Not much.
	What's new?	Nothing.
	How are you doing?	OK.
Less formal	How you doing?	Not bad.
	Long time, no see.	Yeah!

	PRECLOSINGS	RESPONSES
More formal	Well, I'm afraid I have to be going. (I've got to get up early tomorrow.)	Thank you for coming.
	It's been a pleasure.	Yes, I've enjoyed it.
	Thank you for the advice.	My pleasure.
	I really must go now. (stronger)	
	It was nice to see you. (*Note past tense.*)	It was good to see *you*.
	Well, it's getting late.	Maybe we can talk again.
	I know you're busy . . .	
	Nice to see you again.	Nice to see *you*.
	Thanks for coming.	It was fun.
	Maybe we could get together sometime.	Sounds good.
	Great seeing you.	Same here.
Less formal	I've really got to go.	OK. See you.
	Got to go now.	See you again.

	CLOSINGS	RESPONSES
More formal	Until the next time . . .	Good-bye.
	Good night, Bill.	Good night, Jean.
	Good-bye, Harry.	Good-bye, Lisa.
	Have a nice (weekend).	You, too.
Less formal	Talk to you later.	Bye. Take it easy.
	See you later.	So long. Take care.

4 SMALL GROUP PRACTICE

A. Using what you've learned

Directions: For each situation that follows, read the cues given, then discuss the relationship among the speakers and the level of formality. Using this information, complete the dialogues orally with phrases from Section 3 or with any other appropriate response. Example:

A: It was nice seeing you again.

B: *yes, let's do it again.*

A: Bye.

B: *Bye.*

Situation 1

A: Hi, Jack. How are you?
B:
A: Not bad. What's up?
B:

Situation 2

X:
Y: Good morning, Dr. Anthony.
X:
Y:

Situation 3

A: ...Well, that's very interesting but I'm afraid I must _____ .
B: All right. I'll be talking to you again later, maybe?
A:
B:

Situation 4

A: ... and that's just the way it happened.
B: Oh, I almost forgot. I'm supposed to meet _____ .
A:
B:
A:

B. Cued dialogues

Directions: After looking at each situation carefully, discuss with your partner(s) the relationship among the speakers and the appropriate level of formality. Then practice, using any words or expressions appropriate to express the functions given. Your teacher will ask you to perform the dialogue for the class.

Situation 1 (Example)

A and *B* are old friends. They see each other again after four years. *A* has an important meeting and can't talk long. (You can use your real names or made-up names for practicing these situations.)

A	B
1. greets *B*, expresses surprise	1. returns greeting and gestures
Hi, Betty! Haven't seen you in ages!	Oh, hi! It *has* been a long while!
2. asks about *B*'s family	2. answers questions, asks about *A*'s job
How's your family?	John's fine and the kids are doing well in school. I hear you're working for a lawyer.
3. replies to *B*'s question, precloses	3. replies to preclosing, gives closing
Yes, I really like it a lot. In fact, I have do go to work now.	It was great seeing you. Bye!
4. replies to closing	
Bye!	

Situation 2

A and *B* are students at the university. They see each other between classes.

A	*B*
1. greets *B*	1. greets *A*, asks about weekend
2. talks about weekend, asks about *B*'s weekend	2. answers question
3. gives preclosing	3. replies to preclosing
4. closes	4. replies

Situation 3

B is *A*'s boss. *A* needs to leave work early today to see the doctor and approaches *B*, who is working at his or her desk.

A	*B*
1. coughs to get *B*'s attention, greets *B*	1. returns greeting, offers help
2. explains situation, requests permission to leave early	2. asks for reason
3. gives reason	3. gives permission
4. thanks *B*, gives preclosing	4. replies to preclosing
5. closes	5. replies

C. Mini-roleplays

Directions: Discuss the situation with your partner and decide on the proper level of formality. You can use the suggested expressions if you want to. Then practice. When you are ready, perform for the class and discuss your performance with your teacher and classmates.

Roleplay 1

Professor *A* and student *B* meet in the corridor. *B* has a class in another building and is already late, but doesn't want to be rude to Professor *A*, who is very friendly and talkative this morning.

Useful expressions

A	*B*
article on communication	copy it later
get your comments	(chemistry) class

Roleplay 2

A and *B* work for the same insurance company. They see each other at the office after a two-week vacation.

Useful expressions

A	*B*
fantastic trip	stayed home and relaxed
went skiing	played golf

Roleplay 3

You are on your way to the bus stop to go downtown for a show that starts at eight o'clock. It is now seven-thirty, and it takes fifteen minutes to get there. You meet an acquaintance who is obviously glad to see you and wants to talk for a while.

Useful expressions

YOU	*ACQUAINTANCE*
terrible hurry	chat for a bit
last-minute appointment	

Roleplay 4

A has to delay *B* by talking while their friends finish preparations for *B*'s surprise birthday party. *B* tries several preclosings, but *A* doesn't listen.

Useful expressions

A	*B*
Did you hear about...?	late for a date
Just one more thing.	busy
Oh, did you know...?	got to go
great weather	nice to see you
new haircut	

2 Introductions and address systems

When making an introduction in any language, you need to know the formulas and rules for doing it. You also need to know what to call the participants. This lesson will help you to identify given names and surnames (last names) and to decide which form of the name is appropriate to use. You will also learn how introductions are made.

Listen to the following dialogues, paying attention to the introductions and the way people address each other.

1 DIALOGUES 📼

Dialogue A

(*The doorbell rings. Mrs. Carr opens the door.*)
Mrs. Carr: Good evening, George. Come in. How have you been?
George: Just fine, thank you. How are you?
Mrs. Carr: Oh, reasonably well.
George: Mrs. Carr, I would like to introduce a friend of mine, if I
5   may: Albert Douglas. Albert, this is Mrs. Elaine Carr.
Albert: Pleased to meet you, Mrs. Carr.
Mrs. Carr: I've heard so much about you, Mr. Douglas. Please do
             come in. Oh, Richie? Darling, I'd like you to meet some-
             one – a friend of George's.
10 Mr. Carr: Oh, hello, George. Glad you could make it.
             (*He shakes hands with George.*)
George: Hello, Rich. It was very thoughtful of you to invite us.
Mrs. Carr: Yes, darling, as I was saying, this is Albert Douglas.
             (*to Albert*) My husband, Richard.
15 Albert: (*shaking hands with Mr. Carr*) Very nice to meet you,
             Mr. Carr.
Mr. Carr: The pleasure's mine. But call me Rich. Everyone does.
             Mind if I call you Albert?
Albert: Of course not. But just plain "Al" will do.

make it: come

12

Discussion

1. Name the characters in this dialogue. Where are they? What are they doing?
2. There are two introductions here. Find the first one. Who is presented to whom?
3. Where is the second introduction? What words does Mrs. Carr use?
4. How are the two introductions different?
5. What do the different people call each other?
6. What kind of relationships do the various people have?
7. When do they use handshakes?
8. What is the significance of "But call me Rich" in line 17?
9. How would you describe the level of formality in this situation? Which character seems least interested in being formal?

Dialogue B

Mark: This seat taken?
Edward: No, help yourself. Haven't seen you before. You new in engineering?
Mark: Yeah, I just switched majors from computer science – too much math!
Edward: Well, don't expect it to be any better here! What's your name, anyway?
Mark: Mark. What's yours?

13

Edward: Edward, but everybody calls me "Chip."
10 Mark: Chip, huh? Well, I'm not going to tell you what *my* nick-
name is! Oh, here comes the professor. What's his name,
anyway? Scarey, or something like that?
Edward: James Kerry. But we call him "Big Jim" because he's so
short.
15 Mark: To his face?
Edward: No. Are you kidding?

major: major field of study
kidding: joking, making a joke

Discussion

1. Where are Mark and Edward? What are they doing?
2. How old are they?
3. How do they introduce themselves?
4. What do they call their professor?
5. What is the level of formality?
6. Paraphrase the last line of the dialogue.
7. Discuss nicknames in your language as compared with English.

2 INTRODUCTIONS AND THE ADDRESS SYSTEM

Introductions

A formal introduction consists of two parts: giving the names and, if
not provided by the context, some information about the people
being introduced so they will have some common ground to begin a
conversation. This information may include the relationship to the
introducer, as in Dialogue A at the beginning of this unit or Dialogue
C in Unit 1.

In making a formal introduction, one person is first presented to
another: "Mrs. Carr, I would like to introduce my friend, Albert."
"Susie, this is Mike." Albert is presented to Mrs. Carr, Mike to Susie.
In general, subordinates are presented to superiors, men to women,
younger to older. Afterward, the presentation is reversed. "Albert,
Mrs. Carr." "Mike, Susie Johnson." (In Unit 1, it was not very polite
of Jack not to give Mike's last name, but informal relationships sometimes allow for that.)

Men usually shake hands when they are introduced to other men. It
is the woman's choice whether or not to shake hands when introduced to a man, and the man should wait for the woman to offer her
hand. If she offers her hand, shake it. Among professional women it
is becoming more and more common to shake hands. Handshakes
should be firm and brief. Americans regard a firm handshake as a
sign of directness and honesty.

People must sometimes introduce themselves: for example, at a party, in a new class, or in a new neighborhood. If you meet a new neighbor on the same street or in the hallway of your apartment building you might say: "Hello, I'm (full name). I've just moved here." The other person responds by giving his or her full name and indicating where he or she lives.

A reintroduction may occur when two people who have met before see each other again. The reintroduction enables them to converse.

A: I'm (full name). You may not remember, but we met at Sally's.
B: Oh, yes. I remember now. What a party that was!

The address system

In most languages there are specific linguistic features that mark the relationship of the speakers, for example: the *tu/usted/vous* and *du/ni* varieties of the second-person pronoun or the honorifics. In English this relationship is marked by the use of the address system.

Most Americans have three names: a first (sometimes called a given) name, a middle name (or an initial), and a last name (called the family name, or surname). Examples:

James   Arthur Phillips
Barbara Kay   Tillitt
Dan   D.   Newton
Patricia   Redford

As in any language or culture, people who do not know each other well or who differ in status use formal address: title + family (last) name, for example, Dr. Johnson. In universities, some departments insist on formality and the use of title + last name. Others prefer a less formal use of names and titles. Look and listen to the people in your department.

People who know each other well use first names in both informal and formal situations. To change from a formal naming relationship to an informal one, the superior (in age, position, etc.) should suggest it:

A: Why don't you call me Bill?
B: All right, Bill.

This often happens in an informal situation, such as a party or a social event.

	ADDRESS FORMS	FUNCTION
Formal	Dr. Snow Professor Schultz Dean Schoolcraft	*Title + last name* Used in formal situations
	Mr. Carnegie Miss Scaife Mrs. Snow Ms. Newman	*Mr.*: a man *Miss*: a single woman *Mrs.*: a married woman *Ms.*: a single or married woman
	Susan Melanie Barbara Patricia Joseph	*Full first name* Note: Some people want their full first name used in all situations.
Informal	Anderson Smith Pearson Polifroni	*Last name only* Used in sports or in the military, and in some offices. Used by a superior to a subordinate or among equals. Do *not* use this form unless you are certain that it is appropriate.

Sue Barb Pat Joe	*Short first name* Not all names have a short form, but many do.	
Bobby	*Diminutive first name* Some people consider this form childish, so make sure it is appro- priate to use.	
Intimate Red Sunny Chip T.J. Flip	*Nickname* Very informal; should be used only when you are *sure* the per- son wants you to use this form. Some names (such as Red) are very personal and can be insult- ing if not used properly.	

Note: If an American name is new to you, you should find out
whether it is a man's name or a woman's name, to avoid embarrass-
ment to yourself later. A few names (Chris, Pat, Bobby, Terry, etc.)
can refer either to a female or to a male.

	FIRST NAME (FULL)	FIRST NAME (SHORT)	FIRST NAME (DIMINUTIVE)
Female	Barbara	Barb	Barbie
	Catherine, Kathryn	Cathy, Kathy, Kate	Kitty, Katie
	Christina	Chris, Tina	Chrissy
	Jean	Jean	Jeannie
	Patricia	Pat, Trish	Patty, Patti
	Susan, Suzanne	Sue	Susie, Suzy
Male	Alfred	Al	Alfie
	Charles	Chuck	Charlie
	Christopher	Chris	
	David	Dave	Davy, Davie
	James	Jim	Jimmy
	John	Jack	Johnny, Jackie
	Joseph	Joe	Joey
	Patrick	Pat	Paddy
	Robert	Bob, Rob	Bobby, Robby

Discussion

Do you use handshakes or other gestures in introductions? What kind
of titles do you use in formal address in your country? How do you
address teachers? How do teachers address students? A name is often
used to get a person's attention. What other ways of getting attention
can you think of?

3   PHRASES 🔊

Directions: Listen to the following phrases on the tape as you read along here. Then practice saying them. The phrases near the top of the list are generally more formal than the ones near the bottom.

INTRODUCTIONS

	INTRODUCER	RESPONSE A	RESPONSE B
More formal	I'd like to introduce Henry Cheng.	How do you do?	How do you do?
↑	I'd like to introduce Marie Brandon.	Glad to meet you.	The pleasure is mine.
	I'd like you to meet Patricia Murphy.	Nice to meet you.	Nice to meet *you*.
	I'd like to introduce Tony Angelo.	Pleased to meet you.	
Less formal	I'd like you to meet Akiko Sato.	Nice to meet you.	I've heard so much about you.
	This is Ali Hassan.	Hi.	Hi.

SELF-INTRODUCTIONS

	SELF	RESPONSE
More formal	Hello. I'm John du Plessis.	How do you do? I'm Julie Duarte.
	Hello. My name is George Kyrkostas.	Pleased to meet you. I'm Sue Washington.
↕	I don't think we've met. I'm Young Kim.	Nice to meet you. I'm Eva Beck.
Less formal	Hi. I'm Mike. What's your name?	Hi. I'm Margaret, but everyone calls me Peggy.

4 SMALL GROUP PRACTICE

A. Using what you've learned

Directions: For each situation that follows, read the cues given, then discuss the relationship among the speakers and the level of formality. Using this information, complete the dialogues orally with phrases from Section 3 or with any other appropriate response. Example:

A: Bill, this is Joe. He's new in class.

B: *Hi, Joe.*
C: *Hi, Bill.*

Situation 1

A:
B: Nice to meet you, Miss Douglas.
C:
B: I'm a mechanical engineer.
C:
B:

Situation 2

Greg: Susan, I'd like you to meet Alice Carter, a good friend of
       mine.
Susan:
Alice:
Susan: Greg's told me a lot of good things about you, Alice.
Alice:

Situation 3

A: Hi. I guess I don't know you. My name's _____.
B:
A:
B:

Situation 4

A:
B: Pleased to meet you. I'm _____.
A:
B:

B. Cued dialogues

Directions: After looking at each situation carefully, discuss with your partner(s) the relationship among the speakers and the appropriate level of formality. Then practice, using any words or expressions appropriate to express the functions given. Your teacher will ask you to perform the dialogue for the class.

Situation 1

A is a clerk in a large department store. *B* is her boyfriend. *C* works in the department store with *A*. *B* is meeting *A* at the store to go out for lunch.

A	*B*	*C*
1. greets *B*; introduces co-worker, *C*	1. greets *C*	1. returns greeting
2. tells *C* about *B*'s job		2. asks *B* for more details
	3. answers question	

Situation 2

Three university students meet in the hall on their way to class. *A* knows both *B* and *C*, but *B* and *C* don't know each other.

A	*B*	*C*
1. greets *B*	1. greets *A*	
2. introduces *C*	2. greets *C*	2. replies to *B*
	3. asks *C* about his or her classes	3. tells what classes he or she is taking
4. remarks how well *C* is doing in school		

Situation 3

A is taking an introductory course in biochemistry. *A* doesn't know any of the classmates very well and is nervous about an upcoming test. Finally, *A* decides to call another student from the class and ask if they could study together.

A	*B*
	1. answers telephone
2. greets *B* and identifies self	2. greets *A*
3. explains the problem, makes a suggestion	3. accepts suggestion and makes arrangements for the meeting *or* rejects suggestion and gives reason
4. expresses pleasure/thanks *or* expresses regret, gives preclosing	4. replies to preclosing
5. says good-bye	5. says good-bye

C. Mini-roleplays

Directions: Discuss the situation with your partner(s) and decide on the proper level of formality. Then practice. You can use the suggested expressions if you want to. When you are ready, perform for the class and discuss your performance with your teacher and classmates.

Roleplay 1

A and *B* work in the same department. *A* has just started this week. They meet *C*, president of the company, at the water fountain.

Useful expressions

A	*B*	*C*
newest _____	like you to meet	increased productivity

Roleplay 2

A is in a new class at school and wants to make new friends. *A* introduces himself or herself to *B*, who seems to know the way around.

Useful expressions

A	*B*
English, too?	courses are great
have an apartment?	live on campus

Roleplay 3

A is invited to *B*'s house for coffee, but *A* doesn't like *B*. *A* must decide whether or not to accept *B*'s invitation.

Useful expressions

A	*B*
not sure about Saturday	we should get together more often
busy schedule	hope you can come
will let you know for sure	wouldn't be any fun without you

Roleplay 4

A thinks *B* is nice, but they don't know each other very well. *A* invites *B* to a party *A* is having.

Useful expressions

A	*B*
never see you outside of class	always studying
must be a good student	not sure about that
having a party this Saturday	don't dance much
come on over if you can	

3 Invitations

This chapter focuses on social invitations – how to make them and how to respond to them. After completing the exercises, you should feel comfortable in making and replying to invitations in various situations.

When you listen to the following dialogues, listen especially for the ways people make and accept social invitations.

1 DIALOGUES 📼

Dialogue A

(*A knock at the door*)

Gretchen: Good morning, Dr. Hampton. May I come in?

Dr. Hampton: Good morning, Gretchen. Of course. How can I be of help?

Gretchen: Well, it's not about school, Dr. Hampton. It's just that Alan and I wanted to have a few people over for a dinner party to celebrate finishing my dissertation, and we'd like to invite you especially, since you're chairman. Would you be able to come the weekend after next, on Saturday?

Dr. Hampton: I'd be delighted to, Gretchen. Saturday, did you say?

Gretchen: If that's all right for you and Mrs. Hampton.

Dr. Hampton: I'll have to check with Elizabeth, but I'm pretty sure it'll be all right.

Gretchen: Good. If you could come around six-thirty or seven o'clock, that would give us time to chat a while over a glass of wine before dinner.

Dr. Hampton: That sounds fine. We'll be there around seven.

Gretchen: That would be great! Oh, I'm so pleased that you and Mrs. Hampton will be able to make it!

Dr. Hampton: Well, it should be fun. And you deserve it after all that hard work. But, say, Gretchen, will I have to start calling you *Doctor* Schmeltzer now?

Gretchen: Of course not, Dr. Hampton!

Dr. Hampton: Well, then can't you reciprocate by calling me Henry?

Gretchen: Of course, Dr.... I mean *Henry* – but it'll take some getting used to.

dissertation: the big research project paper written by a candidate for the Ph.D. degree.

it'll take some getting used to: it will take some time to get accustomed to

Discussion

1. Describe the speakers' relationship. What forms of address do they use?
2. Where does the conversation take place? What is the topic of conversation?
3. How does Gretchen introduce the invitation? Why is she being so flexible about the time in her invitation?
4. What kind of gathering is it going to be? Is anyone besides Dr. and Mrs. Hampton going to be invited?
5. What is the function of lines 24–26?
6. What do you think the guests will be wearing to the dinner party?
7. How formal is this dialogue?

Dialogue B

(*The telephone rings.*)

Tom: Hello.

Don: Hello, Tom? This is Don. How are you?

Tom: Oh, hi, Don. Good. How have you been?

Don: Fine. Listen, Jerry and I wanted to go bowling tomorrow night
5   out at the bowling alley on seventy-nine, but we don't have a
      way to get there. If you drive, we'll pick up the tab for the
      bowling. How about it?

Tom: Well, it sounds like fun, but actually I've really got a lot of
      homework to do just now.

10 Don: Oh, come on, Tom. It'll be fun. Make you relax. You'll study
      better!

Tom: I really can't. I've got a chemistry exam on Monday and a
      book report due on Tuesday in American Lit. that I'm really
      getting nervous about. I don't think I'd enjoy it much. But
15   thanks a lot for thinking of me. Sorry I can't help you out.

Don: Oh, don't worry about it. Maybe next time. Good luck on
      your exam.

Tom: Thanks. See you.

Don: Bye.

seventy-nine: the name of a highway

pick up the tab: to pay for (a dinner, tickets, etc.)

Discussion

1. Who calls whom on the telephone? Why?
2. What kind of invitation is there?
3. How does Tom react to the invitation? What is his reply?
4. How does Don feel at the end of the conversation?
5. What is the level of formality in this conversation?

Dialogue C

(*The telephone rings.*)

David: Hello?

Cathy: Oh, hello, David. How are you?

David: Just fine, thanks, Cathy.

Cathy: Say, Dick and I were wondering, are you and Shirley free this
5   Friday?

David: Friday? Oh... it seems Shirley mentioned something about
       having to work late on Friday. Why, what did you have in
       mind?

Cathy: Oh, we just thought it would be nice to have you over for
10   dinner, but if you're not available...

David: Well, let me check again with Shirley. I'll call you tonight and
       let you know for sure, OK?

Cathy: All right. I'll be waiting for your call.

David: OK. Till then.

have someone over for dinner: invite someone to dinner at one's home

Discussion

1. Why does Cathy call David?
2. What form of address do the participants use?
3. Notice that Cathy does not identify herself. What could explain this?
4. What can you say about David's attitude toward Cathy in lines 6–8? How eager is he to accept an invitation from Cathy?
5. What is the result of the invitation?

---

2 INVITATIONS

An invitation consists of requesting someone's presence, stating the specific event, and setting the time and place. Spoken invitations are fine for most occasions, but for certain special events, such as weddings, anniversaries, and baby showers, formal written invitations are traditionally sent. They should be answered in writing and returned to the RSVP address. (RSVP stands for *répondez, s'il vous plaît*, a French expression that means you should respond to the invitation by calling or, preferably, writing the host.)

It is fairly common to send printed "party" invitations for large semi-formal cocktail parties. They may say "Regrets only" and give a telephone number at the bottom, which means you call only if you cannot attend.

Making the invitation

People usually do not begin a conversation with an invitation, but instead preface the invitation in some way. (See Dialogue A, lines 4–6.) Once this type of introduction is made, the inviter (the host) is free to make the invitation, in one of two ways:

1. states what kind of party, excursion, etc., is being planned; or
2. asks if the listener is free at such-and-such a time and then says why.

The first invitation is preferable, because it allows the listener to decide whether to accept or not. The second is likely to get an indecisive response, as in Dialogue C, lines 6–8.

Invitations are usually made privately, in person or by phone. That is, only the people being invited hear the invitation. People usually do not feel comfortable inviting you to a party if you are with someone who is not going to be invited. (Dialogue A in Unit 4 gives an example of when it is proper to make an invitation in front of someone who is not invited.)

Accepting the invitation

Accepting invitations is very easy. You thank the person for the invitation or express pleasure at being invited and then get the details of place and time. It is also a good idea to find out just how formally you should dress. Appropriate dress varies according to season and to region.

In many informal cases, you then ask the host or hostess whether you can help by bringing something, such as a bottle of wine. Often the host will thank you for offering but will tell you it isn't necessary. However, guests often bring a gift of wine or flowers, even if the host has turned down an offer at the time of the invitation. A small item from your country would be quite appropriate as such a gift.

If you have children and you have been invited out by an American, you should not bring your children unless they have been specifically invited. In general, evening parties are not appropriate for children, especially if they are small. Picnics and barbecues, on the other hand, are usually good parties for children.

Refusing the invitation

If an invitation must be refused, most people expect a reason. The following sequence would be appropriate: apology, reason for refusal, thanks for the invitation, and perhaps a second apology (see Dialogue B).

If someone asks if you are free at a certain time, but doesn't say what the invitation is for, you are not required to commit yourself until you know what the invitation is for. For example, if you say that you're free and the invitation turns out to be something you'd hate to do (a trip to a local sight you've seen ten times), then you will be in a position of having to take back your acceptance or of inventing an excuse later. If this happens, tell the person who invited you that you have to check and that you'll tell him or her later.

Non-invitations

There are also phrases that sound like invitations but in fact are not. People may say things like: "We'll have to get together sometime" or "You'll have to come over and visit us sometime." You can identify such non-invitations by their generality – there is *no specific time mentioned*, and the word "sometime" is often used. They are often ritual expressions of parting. On these occasions you could respond: "Yes, that would be nice," or "I'd love to," or something similar, and then let the subject drop. If they do not call you, you could always invite them for some occasion.

Problems with invitations

When someone asks you to his or her home, it is very clear who is the guest and who is the host, but invitations to restaurants for lunch, dinner, coffee, a drink, etc., sometimes present problems, and the customs vary in different parts of the United States.

In many instances it is the inviter who pays, as one would expect, but in some instances each one pays his or her own check: You "go dutch." This is often the case with friends in informal situations, such as "Let's go get a beer" or "Want a cup of coffee?" In some parts of the country, however, some people like to entertain friends by taking them to a restaurant for dinner instead of having dinner at home. In this case the host expects to pay and the guest may offer to leave the tip, which may be declined by the host. (If so, just let the matter drop.) If the invitation is expressed in fairly casual terms, such as "Let's go to (name of restaurant) for dinner," it may be more of a suggestion than an invitation, so you should be prepared to pay your part of the bill.

If you want to invite someone for a meal at a restaurant, be explicit: "I'd like to take you to..." Americans should be explicit also, but they often assume you know the local customs in the matter. Ask a friend's advice if you are not sure.

Discussion

Is it acceptable to refuse an invitation in your country? Under what circumstances? Do people use "non-invitations"? When going out to a restaurant or movie, is it common in your country to "go dutch"?

3 PHRASES 🔲

Directions: Listen to the following phrases on the tape as you read along here. Then practice saying them. The phrases near the top of the list are generally more formal than the ones near the bottom.

	MAKING AN INVITATION	ACCEPTING	REFUSING
More formal	I'd like to invite you to dinner this Saturday.	Thank you. I'd love to.	I'm awfully sorry, but I have other plans.
	I'd like to invite you to a party next Friday.	That would be wonderful.	I wish I could, but...
	I was wondering if you'd like to...	Yes, thank you. What time?	I'd really like to, but...
	We're going to have a few friends over on Wednesday, and we'd love you to come.		
	Are you free on Saturday? Would you like to...	Thanks. I'd love to.	Sorry. I've already made plans for Saturday.
	How about dinner?	Sounds great.	Oh darn! Have to...
	How about coffee?	OK.	
Less formal	Let's go to our place for a beer.	All right.	

	OFFERING TO BRING SOMETHING	RESPONSE
More formal	I wonder if I might be able to bring something?	It's enough just to have you come.
	Let me bring something, won't you?	Oh, you don't need to.
	Is there anything I could bring?	
	What shall I bring?	Just bring yourself.
	Can I bring the wine?	Well, thanks, if you'd like to.
Less formal	What should I bring?	Well, John's bringing salad, so why don't you bring dessert?

MAKING A NON-INVITATION

You'll have to come over sometime.
We'll have to get together again soon.
If you're ever in Houston, look me up.
If you're ever in Pittsburgh, give me a call.
If you're ever in the area, come and visit.

4 SMALL GROUP PRACTICE

A. Using what you've learned

Directions: For each situation that follows, read the cues given and discuss the relationship between the speakers and the level of formality. Using this information, complete the dialogues orally using phrases from Section 3 or with any other appropriate response. Example:

A: Can you come for dinner Sunday?

B: *I'd love to. What can I bring?*

A: Some white wine would be fine.

B: *OK. See you then. Thanks.*

Situation 1

A: Would you like to come over for dinner tomorrow?
B: _____. What time?
A:
B:

Situation 2

A:
B: Oh, that would be great! _____?
A: Around eight o'clock.
B:
A:

Situation 3

A:
B: Well, I had planned to go see a movie that night. Why?
A:
B:

Situation 4

A:
B: Oh, I'm sorry, but _____.
A:
B:

B. Cued dialogues

Directions: After looking at each situation carefully, discuss with your partner(s) the relationship among the speakers and the appropriate level of formality. Then practice, using any words or expressions appropriate to express the functions given. Your teacher will ask you to perform the dialogue for the class.

Situation 1

A and *B* are good friends. They work in the same office. *A* has just finished moving into a new house and wants to invite *B* over to celebrate.

A	*B*
1. greets *B*	1. returns greeting
2. invites *B* to housewarming	2. accepts invitation, asks about time
3. gives time	3. offers to bring something
4. accepts *or* rejects the offer	4. expresses pleasure, thanks *A* for invitation

housewarming: party to celebrate moving into a new house

Situation 2

A is a professor at a large university where *B*, a foreign student, is a candidate for the Ph.D. degree. *A* and *B* have met each other only once before. Now *A* wants to invite *B* to his or her house for a barbecue.

A	*B*
1. greets *B*	1. greets *A*
2. invites *B*	2. asks about time
3. gives time	3. accepts invitation, thanks *A*
4. expresses pleasure	

Situation 3

A and *B* are both students in the same English class, but from different countries. They don't know each other very well, but *A* hopes that by inviting *B* over for dinner, they can become better acquainted.

A	*B*
1. greets *B*	1. greets *A*
2. invites *B*	2. accepts invitation
3. gives time and location	3. disagrees with the time, suggests alternate time
4. agrees	4. expresses pleasure, thanks *A*
5. acknowledges thanks, gives directions to location	

31

Situation 4

A works for a large corporation. *B* is *A*'s boss, but the two don't know each other very well. *A* decides to invite the boss (with husband or wife) to dinner.

A	*B*
1. greets *B*	1. greets *A*, asks what *A* wants
2. invites *B*	2. asks for more information
3. gives information	3. accepts invitation *or* rejects invitation and gives reason
4. expresses pleasure *or* expresses regret	

C. Mini-roleplays

Directions: Discuss the situation with your partner(s) and decide on
the proper level of formality. You can use the suggested expressions if
you want to. Then practice. When you are ready, perform for the
class and discuss your performance with your teacher and classmates.

Roleplay 1

A and a friend, *B*, are standing in the hall talking. *C* comes up to
them and greets them. *C* wants to invite *A* to a dinner party, but
doesn't want *B* to come.

Useful expressions

A	C	B

nice to see you again
we were just talking
	what's happening?
	just passing by
	give me a call, *A*
		haven't seen you in a
		   long time
		I think she's avoiding
		   me

Roleplay 2

Student *A* wants to invite Professor *B* to dinner, but *B*'s schedule is
very full.

Useful expressions

A	B
come over for dinner love to have you	awfully busy schedule reports to write for the president

4 Thanking people and replying to thanks

In this unit, we will look at and practice situations that require an expression of thanks. As you proceed through the unit, you may notice situations that in your native culture do not require a thank-you. You may also notice situations where a thank-you would be expected in your country, but not expected in the United States.

Listen to the dialogues, paying particular attention to when people say thank you and to *what* they say to express thanks. Also notice what the person being thanked says in reply. Then discuss the questions at the end of each dialogue.

1 DIALOGUES

Dialogue A

Harry Carpenter:	(*Crossing the room to where Mrs. King is standing talking to another guest*) Excuse me, Marilyn? It's getting late, so I'm afraid we'll have to be leaving.
Marilyn King:	Oh, so early?
5 Louise Carpenter:	Well, Harry's got to get up and drive to the airport for an eight o'clock plane tomorrow.
Harry:	We've really had a wonderful time, Marilyn. Thank you very much for inviting us.
Marilyn:	Say, Louise, why don't we meet downtown for lunch some day next week?
10 Louise:	I'd love to!
Marilyn:	I've heard Harold's has delicious salads.
Louise:	Oh! That sounds wonderful.
Marilyn:	I'll give you a call later on and we can decide the time.
15 Harry:	Honey?
Louise:	All right, dear. Well, it's been a delightful evening. Thank you very much.
Marilyn:	Not at all.
20 Louise:	I'll look forward to your phone call.
Harry:	Thanks again. Good night.
Marilyn:	Good night.
Louise:	Good night.

Discussion

1. Describe the setting.
2. What does "giving someone a call" mean (see line 14)?
3. Paraphrase Harry's remark in line 16.
4. Identify the preclosings. Find the expressions of thanks.
5. How formal is this dialogue?

Dialogue B

(*The telephone rings.*)

Ella: Hello?

Susan: Ella? Susan. How are you?

Ella: Oh, hi, Susan. What's up?

Susan: I just wanted to thank you again for the towels. When I got
5 home from the shower I checked, and they just match our
curtains.

Ella: Oh, don't mention it. You deserve a few towels for putting up
with that guy of yours!

Susan: Yeah, he's something else.

10 Ella: Seriously, though, I wish you all the happiness in the world.

Susan: Thank you, I know you do. That's sweet of you. Well, I suppose I'd better get going on my list of errands – got to call the
bakery or there won't be a wedding cake!

Ella: Well, let me know if I can be of any help.

15 Susan: Thanks. I might take you up on that.

Ella: OK. We'll see you later.

Susan: Yeah. And thanks again. Bye.

Ella: Bye-bye.

shower: a party for someone who is getting married or having a baby
put up with: endure

Discussion

1. How many expressions of thanks are there in this dialogue? How
   do they differ?
2. Who decides to end the conversation? Note that usually the person
   who initiates a telephone conversation will also make the decision
   to end it.
3. Describe the relationship between the two women.
4. Point out which expressions show that this is an informal
   conversation.
5. How would Susan say the first line if she were speaking to someone in a formal context?

Dialogue C

> (*The doorbell rings.*)

Linda: Oh, hi, welcome back! Have a nice trip?

Janet: Oh, it was fantastic! Fresh air and sunshine every day. We were really lucky with the weather.

Linda: Come on in. I've got the coffeepot on.

5   Janet: Thanks, but I've got a ton of laundry to do. I just stopped by with this – it's for you.

Linda: Oh, thank you! It's beautiful! I don't have any plants like this. But you shouldn't have.

Janet: Well, Jim and I just wanted to show you how much we

10   appreciated your looking after the house and watering the plants while we were away.

Linda: Well, what are friends for? By the way, I tried to buy you those towels you wanted on sale, but they only had these really ugly ones left. Sorry.

15   Janet: Oh, that's OK. Thanks for trying.

Linda: You're welcome.

Discussion

1. Where does the conversation take place?
2. Does Janet express thanks in line 5? What else does she express?
3. Why does Linda thank Janet in line 7?
4. Paraphrase line 8.
5. Identify the two speakers' relationship and the level of formality.

2 THANKING PEOPLE AND REPLYING TO THANKS

As you know, there are many different situations that call for an expression of thanks. As in the case of invitations, it is sometimes appropriate to send formal, *written* thank-you letters and cards. In this unit, however, we will be concerned only with spoken language.

When to thank

The following list contains the most common situations that require thanks. You may be able to think of other ones as well. In general, people thank someone:

1. for a gift;
2. for a favor;
3. for an offer of help;
4. for a compliment and a wish of success;
5. when asked about their health;
6. for an invitation;
7. when leaving a party or social gathering;
8. for services, such as being waited on in a store or restaurant.

Thanking for gifts

There is a specific form for this type of thank-you (see Dialogues B and C). The person receiving the gift usually says three things:

1. an expression of thanks;
2. a compliment on the gift itself, showing that the recipient likes the gift; and
3. a question relating to the gift (its origin, use, maker, etc.) to show interest in the gift. This is really another type of compliment (Unit 7) and is optional in informal circumstances.

Two examples of thanking are:

Janice: Oh, thank you! I just love roses! Are they from your garden?

Jack: It's beautiful! Thank you very much. I've always wanted a picture from Japan. Did you get it in Osaka?

Another way of thanking for a gift is to use an expression of thanks and then to state that a gift was not necessary or expected:

Mike: Oh, thank you. But you really didn't have to.

Note: Although people do telephone to thank for a gift, a written note is also expected.

Thanking for favors

A "favor" is doing something for another person that the doer had no obligation to do, for example, going to the store for a friend or mailing some letters so that a sick friend wouldn't have to go out in the rain. Since a favor involves doing something *extra*, it requires an expression of thanks. In Dialogue C, Linda has done a favor for Janet. Janet thanks Linda by giving her a plant as a present.

Two ways of offering a favor and asking for a favor are:

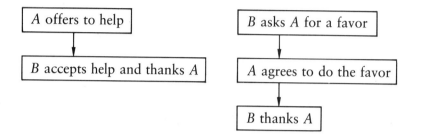

It is appropriate to thank the person again after the favor has been done. For "bigger" favors, that is, ones involving more time or effort, the beneficiary (*B*, above) may also give a gift to the doer of the favor (*A*, above). For small things, such as holding open a door, a person simply says "Thanks" and the response is usually the nasal sound "Mm-hmm."

Thanking for offers of help

Always thank someone who offers to help you, whether you accept their help or refuse it politely (see Dialogue B). When refusing an offer of help, you may want to say something like:

No, thank you.
No, but thank you for offering.
Thank you, but I'll manage OK by myself.

Nick: Do you need help moving this weekend?
Joe: Thanks, I've already got four other guys! But thanks for offering.

Remember that in the U.S., offers of help are usually made only once. Therefore, do not politely refuse the first time thinking you will be asked again.

Thanking for compliments and wishes of success

When you receive a compliment, whether on your work, your clothing, your family, or anything else, it is appropriate to say thank you, and to make a comment about the thing being complimented. (Making and replying to compliments will be discussed in more detail in Unit 7.)

Nancy: That's a nice shirt!
Rolando: Oh, thanks. I just got it at Sears.

David: You're a good driver.
Liz: Thanks. I had a good teacher.

Americans also say thank you when someone wishes them well (see Dialogue B).

Steve: Good luck on your exam tomorrow, Sal.
Sal: Thanks, Steve. I'll need it!

Thanking for interest in your health

"Thank you" is also used in reply to questions about your health, or that of a relative.

Mark: How's your husband these days?
Ellen: Oh, he's pretty good, thanks.

Thanking for invitations

In Unit 3 you practiced thanking for invitations. Remember that it is polite to thank the other person for the invitation, whether or not you accept it.

Peggy: Can you come over for lunch on Saturday?
Molly: Oh, I'd love to, but I've got a dentist's appointment at eleven-thirty. Thanks anyway for the invitation.

Thanking when leaving a party

Expressions of thanks are always made when the guests take leave of the host. At this time, the host may reply by thanking the guests for coming, saying that it was nice to have had them over (see Dialogue A).

Mrs. Downes: Thank you so much for the lovely evening, Charlotte. Frank and I had such a good time.

Mrs. Hill: You're quite welcome, Mildred. Thank *you* for coming. We'd been looking forward to seeing you for a long time.

Thanking for other services

Americans often thank each other at other times, too. A student may thank a professor who has just written comments on one of the student's papers or who had taken the time to see the student, in spite of a very full schedule. Patients will also thank doctors for their services.

Doctor: . . . so the best thing now is to go home and take these pills, and if you don't feel better in a couple of days, let me know.

Patient: Thank you very much, Doctor.

Doctor: That's quite all right. Good-bye.

In a store, the clerk thanks the customer for making the purchase and the customer thanks the clerk for helping.

Clerk: There you are. Thank you.

Customer: (*taking the package*) Thank you.

In a restaurant, the waiter or waitress thanks the customer when the order is taken, and the customer sometimes thanks the waiter or waitress as each course is placed on the table.

Waiter: Are you ready to order?

Customer: Yes, I'll have. . .

Waiter: Thank you.
(*Waiter puts down the drinks.*)

Customer: Thank you.

Discussion

Are there times when your culture requires an expression of thanks, but American culture does not? Is it common to give gifts as an expression of thanks?

3 PHRASES 🔲

Directions: Listen to the following phrases on the tape as you read along here. Then practice saying them. The phrases near the top of the list are generally more formal than the ones near the bottom.

	EXPRESSING THANKS	RESPONSE
More formal	I'm very grateful for...	You're very welcome.
	I'm very grateful for...	You're quite welcome.
	I'm so grateful for ...	You're entirely welcome.
	Thank you very much for...	Don't mention it.
	Thank you so much for...	You're welcome.
	Thank you for ...	It was my pleasure.
	That was nice of you. Thank you.	Don't mention it.
	That was nice of you.	You're welcome.
	Thank you. But you really shouldn't have.	Well, I just wanted to show my appreciation for ...
	They're beautiful! But you didn't need to (give me anything).	But I wanted to.
	Thanks a lot for...	You're welcome.
	I really appreciate (the invitation).	Sure.
	Thanks!	It was nothing. What are friends for?
Less formal	Thanks a million!	Don't worry about it.
	Thanks a million!	Forget it.

	EXPRESSING THANKS FOR A FAILED ATTEMPT	RESPONSE
More formal	Thank you for trying.	I'm sorry it didn't work out.
	I appreciate your help, anyway.	Perhaps you'll have better luck next time.
	Thank you very much for your efforts.	
Less formal	Thanks, anyway.	Sorry it didn't work out.
	Thanks a lot for trying, at least.	Sure. Too bad it didn't work.

4 SMALL GROUP PRACTICE

A. Using what you've learned

Directions: For each situation that follows, read the cues given, then discuss the relationship among the speakers and the level of formality. Using this information, complete the dialogues orally with phrases from Section 3 or with any other appropriate response. Example:

A: Thanks a lot. The flowers are beautiful.

B: *You're welcome. I'm glad you like them.*

Situation 1

A: I would like to take this opportunity to thank you for _____.
B:
A:

Situation 2

A:
B: _____, but you really shouldn't have.
A:
B:

Situation 3

A: I'm very grateful to you for _____.
B:
A:
B:

Situation 4

A: Thanks a lot for _____.
B:

B. Cued dialogues

Directions: After looking at each situation carefully, discuss with your partner the relationship among the speakers and the appropriate level of formality. Then practice, using any words or expressions appropriate to express the functions given. Your teacher will ask you to perform the dialogue for the class.

Situation 1

A has just recently gotten married to *B*'s former roommate. *A* sees *B* at the bookstore and goes over to thank *B* for the wedding gift.

A	*B*
1. greets *B*	1. greets *A*
2. thanks *B* for the present, compliments *B* on the gift	2. replies to thanks
3. asks for more information about the gift	3. replies to question
4. repeats thanks, compliments present again	4. replies to compliment
5. gives preclosing	5. replies to preclosing
6. says good-bye	6. says good-bye

Situation 2

Same circumtances as in Situation 1, except that now *B* is *A*'s academic adviser at the university. *A* doesn't know *B* very well, and is a little nervous. *A* drops by *B*'s office to thank *B* again for the gift. (Use the functions in Situation 1.)

Situation 3

A is going to move and needs a lot of help. *A* talks to friend *B* before class that day.

A	*B*
1. greets *B*	1. greets *A*, asks about *A*'s family
2. thanks *B* and gives information, asks *B* to do a favor	2. agrees to do the favor *or* refuses to do the favor and gives an excuse, wishes *A* well
3. thanks *B*, makes arrangements, gives preclosing *or* thanks *B*, expresses regret, gives preclosing	3. replies to preclosing
4. says good-bye	4. says good-bye

C. Mini-roleplays

Directions: Discuss the situation with your partner and decide on the proper level of formality. You can use the suggested expressions if you want to. Then practice. When you are ready, perform for the class and discuss your performance with your teacher and classmates.

Roleplay 1

X needs someone to babysit while he or she goes to a doctor's appointment. X calls friend Y and asks Y to do this favor. Y either agrees to do it or refuses to and gives the reason. After arrangements are made, they say good-bye and hang up.

Useful expressions

X	Y
doctor's appointment at _____ o'clock	what can I do for you?
really would appreciate the favor	always glad to be of help
shouldn't take more than _____ minutes	what are friends for?
	sorry, but I've got to...

Roleplay 2

X just got an exam back and got a poor grade on it. X is very worried and asks the professor for an appointment to talk about it. The professor has a very busy schedule but manages to find a time to meet. After making arrangements, X says good-bye.

Useful expressions

X	PROFESSOR Z
really worried about my test	you do need some help
don't understand these problems	I'm glad you're taking this seriously
make an appointment to talk	my schedule is rather full just now
whenever it's convenient for you	what about (day and time)
thank you	you're welcome

Roleplay 3

A, B's boss, wants to invite B to a formal dinner party. B wants to go but isn't sure how to get there or what to wear.

Useful expressions

A	B
dinner party at my house	I would be delighted to
just a few business associates	rather formal?
wear a dark suit and tie	I've never been to your house…
I'll draw you a map	thank you
	looking forward to (meeting your wife)

5 Apologizing

Everyone makes mistakes, and everyone needs to know what to do and say after making a mistake. This unit focuses on apologies, and the aim is to help you know both *what* to say and *when* to say it.

Listen to the following dialogues and be prepared to answer the discussion questions in class. Listen especially for the occasions when you hear people apologizing. Try to figure out when they apologize and what they say when they apologize.

1 DIALOGUES 📼

Dialogue A

(*The telephone rings.*)
Russell: Hello?
Sandy: Hi, Russ? It's me. Look, we're having a bit of trouble with the car, so it looks like we won't be able to make it tonight. I'm really sorry.
5 Russell: Oh really? What is it?
Sandy: Well, it's the carburetor again. We just had it fixed last week, but it must be clogged up again somehow.
Russell: Well, I'm sorry to hear that. Want me to come get you?
Sandy: Well, actually, we're stuck on the freeway and I had to walk
10 a mile to this gas station to get help.
Russell: In this terrible weather?
Sandy: Yeah, I'm pretty wet, I can tell you that!
Russell: Look, why don't I come pick you guys up in my car, once they tow the car to the station. Where are you at?
15 Sandy: You know that Arco station at the entrance to the freeway?
Russell: Oh, yeah, I know where that is. I'll be right down. We still might be able to catch the late show.
Sandy: OK, great. Sorry about the inconvenience.
Russell: Don't worry about it. See you in a little bit.
20 Sandy: Thanks. See you.

freeway: major highway
inconvenience: trouble

Discussion

1. Where are the two speakers in this dialogue?
2. What is the weather like?
3. What is wrong?
4. What had Sandy, Russell, and the third person referred to in the dialogue been planning to do before the car broke down?
5. What does Sandy apologize for? What words does he use? There are two apologies in this dialogue. Find them both.
6. When Russell says he is sorry (line 8), is this an apology?
7. What does Russell offer to do? What is Sandy's reply?
8. Note that in line 14 the word "at" is not necessary. In standard formal English it would not be appropriate. Why is it used here?

Dialogue B

It is extremely crowded in the cafeteria. Sandra, wearing a backpack, has her arms full of library books and is carrying an umbrella over her arm. She sees a free spot at a table on the other side of the room.

Sandra: (*bumping the pack into someone*) I'm sorry. It's so crowded today.
Person 1: Yeah. It's OK.
Sandra: (*stepping on someone's books*) Oops, sorry.
Person 2: No harm done.
Sandra: (*poking someone with the umbrella*) Oh, I'm so sorry.
Person 3: Maybe you should have left that stuff outside.

	Sandra:	You're right. I'll never try this again. But all the lockers were full.
10	Person 3:	I can see you've got a problem.
	Sandra:	(*putting her books at the empty place*) Is this place free?
	Person 4:	As a matter of fact, this guy asked me to save it for him.
	Person 5:	Yeah, that's my place.
	Sandra:	Oh, I'm sorry. I didn't see anyone here. (*picks up her*
15		*books*)
	Person 5:	No. That's OK. You take it. It'll be easier for *me* to move.
	Sandra:	You're sure? Thanks a lot.

Discussion

1. Why does Sandra apologize so often? How many times does she apologize?
2. Are the apologies different? Why?

Dialogue C

Jeffrey and Paul, roommates at college, are visiting their hometown during spring break. Jeffrey has just told a neighbor, Mrs. Wallace, about Paul's new job after graduation. He also told her how much Paul was going to be earning...

	Paul:	Aw, Jeffrey! What did you have to go and do that for?
	Jeffrey:	Do what?
	Paul:	*You* know what I'm talking about. Why did you go tell Mrs. Wallace how much money I'm going to make? Now she'll go
5		and tell the whole world!
	Jeffrey:	Well, I'm sorry.
	Paul:	Yeah, but you *know* how she talks to everybody and their brother!
	Jeffrey:	Well, I apologize. I guess I wasn't thinking. I got all excited.
10	Paul:	Oh well, it's done now. I guess it doesn't matter that much, anyway. They were bound to find out eventually. Everybody in this town's got a big nose!
	Jeffrey:	You know, it *is* a lot of money for a first job...
	Paul:	You think I'll be able to buy a Porsche?
15	Jeffrey:	Well, I think you'd better wait and see how much is left after Uncle Sam gets *his* share!

Discussion

1. What is Paul's complaint?
2. Which lines constitute the apology? What excuses are given?
3. How does Paul reply to the apology?
4. What does Paul mean about people having big noses (line 12)?
5. Who is Uncle Sam?

2 APOLOGIZING

Usually, you apologize if you have violated a social rule or have done something that hurts or inconveniences another person. The function of the apology is to show regret for the wrongdoing and to offer an explanation or a remedy.

The form

Apologies vary, depending on the formality of the situation, the relationship between the two people, and, most important, the seriousness of the mistake. Stepping on someone's toe accidentally would not require the same type of apology as running over someone's dog in the street. In general, the more serious the error, the more elaborate the apology should be. There are five possible parts to an apology:

1. Formal expression of regret. This may be explicit, as in "I'm sorry," or implied, as in "I didn't mean to."
2. Explanation (excuse), which shows why the mistake occurred.
3. Offer to remedy the situation, if some damage has been done, or a remedy is possible.
4. Assurance that the mistake will not be repeated (for example, subordinate to superior).
5. Admission of guilt, which shows that the person apologizing accepts the blame.

The first part, the formal expression of regret, is almost always included in the apology. The other parts (2–5) can be combined with 1 in various ways, as the following examples indicate. Note, however, that the more serious the infraction, the more of these parts (2–5) will be included:

A: I'm sorry I was late to class, Dr. Paulston, but I overslept.
B: Well, it's OK this time, but you know it's disturbing for the rest of the class.
A: Yes, I know. You're right. I won't let it happen again.

A: Oh, sorry. I didn't know you were sitting here. Let me move my stuff to another table.
B: No, it's OK. I can sit over here just as easily.

A: While you were out I borrowed your coffee cup and I'm afraid I broke it.

When to apologize

There are many different situations that require an apology, but they all have something in common: something undesirable or uncomfortable has happened. Almost always, it is the person who has made the mistake who apologizes. Americans apologize for:

hurting someone's feelings or causing a misunderstanding;
being late for or missing a meeting, class, appointment, etc.;
interrupting a conversation or meeting (see Unit 8);
taking someone else's property by mistake;
being impolite;
damaging another person's property;
telling a secret accidentally ("letting the cat out of the bag");
calling someone early in the morning or late at night;
dialing a wrong number on the telephone;
invading someone's personal space by bumping or hitting them
    accidentally.

In addition, Americans also apologize when some person or animal for whom they have responsibility (their children, guests, relatives, or pets) makes a social error.

Other uses of "I'm sorry"

The words "I'm sorry" do not always indicate an apology. These words are also used to express sympathy, as in "I'm sorry to tell you that you'll have to re-type this report. Mr. Lockhart can't stand spelling errors."

    There are still other situations in which people say "I'm sorry" or "Excuse me" but are not really apologizing. You can use these two expressions if you walk between two people talking in the hallway, or if you cough, burp, sneeze, hiccup, or yawn. You can also say "Pardon me" in a more formal situation. Example:

A: Well, I'm really sorry that your report got coffee spilled on it, but I haven't even been *near* your desk this morning. Can't you write a note to the boss and explain what happened?

Responding to an apology

When someone has done something wrong and has apologized to you for the inconvenience or hurt, you can accept the apology by saying something like: "That's OK" or "It couldn't be helped." (See other phrases in the next section.) When you accept an apology in this manner, you are showing that everything is all right and that you have no hard feelings toward that person. In certain cases, a person will continue to be angry even though the other person has apologized, or may even refuse to accept the apology by saying that there was "no excuse" for the behavior of the other person. This, however, is not the usual way to react to an apology.

Discussion

Have you noticed any times when your culture would have required an apology but American rules did not? How do you feel when someone should apologize to you but does not? Are there ways other than using words that you can apologize?

3 PHRASES 📼

Directions: Listen to the following phrases on the tape as you read along here. Then practice saying them. The phrases near the top of the list are generally more formal than the ones near the bottom.

	APOLOGY	RESPONSE
More formal	Forgive me. I'm terribly sorry about...	That's quite all right.
	Forgive me. I'm terribly sorry about ...	I understand completely.
	Please accept my apologies for ...	You really don't have anything to apologize for.
	Please excuse (my dog).	You don't need to apologize.
	I would like to apologize for ...	I wouldn't worry about it if I were you.
	I apologize for...	Oh that's all right. It can happen to anyone.
	I apologize for...	It's not your fault.
	I apologize for...	Oh, well, that's life.
	I'm sorry. I didn't mean to...	Don't worry about it.
	I'm sorry. I didn't mean to...	It's OK.
	I'm sorry. I didn't mean to...	That's OK.
	Oh no! Did I do that? I'm sorry.	It's OK.
	Oh! Sorry!	No problem.
Less formal	Sorry about that.	Forget it.
	Oops.	

4 SMALL GROUP PRACTICE

A. Using what you've learned

Directions: For each situation that follows, read the cues given, then discuss the relationship among the speakers and the level of formality. Using this information, complete the dialogues orally with phrases from Section 3 or with any other appropriate response. Example:

A: Professor Jones? I would like to apologize for *being late to class*.

B: *It's OK this time. Please be on time in future.*

A: Oh, yes, I will.

Situation 1

A:
B:
A: That's very nice of you. But at least let me pay for the damage.

Situation 2

A: Oh! Was that *your* apple?
B:
A:
B:

Situation 3

A:
B: You really don't need to apologize.
A:

Situation 4

A: Gosh, I'm sorry.
B:

B. Cued dialogues

Directions: After looking at each situation carefully, discuss with your partner the relationship among the speakers and the appropriate level of formality. Then practice, using any words or expressions appropriate to express the functions given. Your teacher will ask you to perform the dialogue for the class.

Situation 1

A was supposed to meet *B* at the country club to play golf. *A* arrived at ten o'clock, waited 45 minutes, and then left. Now *A* sees *B* at the shopping center and goes over to talk with him or her.

A	*B*
1. greets *B*	1. greets *A*
2. asks *B* for an explanation	2. apologizes for not coming, gives explanation
3. replies to *B*'s apology	3. reassures *A* that it won't happen again
4. asks for a new time	4. suggests a time
5. disagrees with time	5. agrees to *A*'s suggestion
6. gives preclosing	6. repeats apology
7. replies to apology, says good-bye	7. says good-bye

Situation 2

A has taken a three-year-old daughter to visit an elderly friend, *B*, who has a house full of antiques. The child has been playing with the pet cat in another room when they hear a crash. *A* and *B* rush to the room to find a vase on the floor and the cat and the child on the table.

A	*B*
1. expresses shock, scolds child, apologizes	1. expresses doubt as to whether it was the fault of the cat or the child
2. offers to pay	2. refuses, repeats doubt
3. repeats apology	3. accepts apology
4. repeats offer to pay	4. refuses

Situation 3

B, an actor in a local play, wants to invite *A*, a friend of a friend, to see the opening-night performance. *B* calls *A* at home to see if *A* can come.

A	*B*
1. answers phone	1. asks to speak with *A*
2. identifies self	2. identifies self, explains how *B* got the number, invites *A*
3. asks for more information	3. gives time and theater
4. declines invitation, apologizes	4. expresses disappointment, tries to persuade *A*
5. repeats apology	5. accepts apology, gives preclosing
6. says good-bye	6. says good-bye

C. Mini-roleplays

Directions: Discuss the situation with your partner(s) and decide on the proper level of formality. You can use the suggested expressions if you want to. Then practice. When you are ready, perform for the class and discuss your performance with your teacher and classmates.

Roleplay 1

A is in a bad mood today because *A*'s favorite football team lost their game last night and will not go to the Super Bowl (a national professional football competition). *B* enters *A*'s office to ask a question, and *A* is rather rude with *B*, but then realizes it and apologizes.

Useful expressions

A	*B*
end of the season	too bad
lousy mood	don't follow football

Roleplay 2

A is a guest at a dinner party that *B* is giving. The guests have just been served the dessert when *A* gets a serious attack of the hiccups. *A* keeps apologizing, but there doesn't seem to be any way to stop them. *C*, another guest at the party, tries to give *A* help, as does *B*. They both have some suggestions for getting rid of the hiccups.

Useful expressions

A	*B*	*C*
this is terrible	drink of water	spoonful of sugar
	breathe in a paper bag	hold your nose and take a drink

Roleplay 3

Two faculty members, *A* and *B*, are standing in the hallway having a discussion when *C* approaches them. *C* needs to talk with *A* very briefly to give *A* a message.

Useful expressions

A	*B*	*C*
agenda for the faculty meeting	new position in the department	message about your class cancelled due to bad weather

Roleplay 4

X has borrowed *Y*'s math textbook over the weekend to study for an exam. Now *X* is returning the book, but notices that some of the pages are torn out, and *X* thinks of the 2-year-old child at home.

Useful expressions

X	*Y*
book-eating monster order a new book	4-year-olds are worse – stronger and faster won't use it any more

6 Expressing anger and resolving conflict

You may have heard Americans expressing their anger and been unsure of what they were saying, because they were talking so fast. Or perhaps you didn't understand why they were angry. In this unit, we will study what makes Americans angry and how they express their anger. You will also learn the acceptable ways of reacting to someone else's anger.

Listen to the dialogues that follow, listening especially for the expressions of anger and the response of the other person in the dialogue. Note also what makes the person angry in the first place.

1 DIALOGUES 📼

Dialogue A

Mr. Sorensen:	Richard, what's that under your paper?
Richard:	What's what?
Mr. Sorensen:	Lift up your arm. What's this?
Richard:	Oh, that. Uh, that's a grocery list. I've got to pick up
	some things on my way home.
Mr. Sorensen:	Do you really expect me to believe that?
Richard:	Well, that's what it is.
Mr. Sorensen:	(*reading*) Soren Kierkegaard, Denmark, 1800s, Hegel, Germany, Sartre, Paris, 1900s... An interesting "grocery" list, Mister Jackson!
Richard:	Oh, gee, let me see that. Oh, my gosh, they must be my notes. How did they get here?
Mr. Sorensen:	I'd like to see you in my office, please. (*They leave the classroom and go to the office down the hall.*) Now, Richard, would you care to explain how the answers to the test questions appeared on your desk?
Richard:	I can't, sir. Someone must have left them on my desk.
Mr. Sorensen:	Someone left them on your desk! Someone with handwriting identical to yours left them on your desk? I'm afraid I can't accept that answer.
Richard:	Are you accusing *me* of cheating?
Mr. Sorensen:	Yes, I am.
Richard:	You can't do that without proof! I'm going to call my counselor!

25   Mr. Sorensen: By all means, do that. In the meantime, however,
                           don't come to class again. I am extremely disap-
                           pointed in your behavior.
      Richard: (*grumbling to himself as he leaves*) What a pig-headed,
                           narrow-minded jerk!

Discussion

1. Where are the two speakers, and what is their relationship?
2. Paraphrase Mr. Sorensen's words in line 6.
3. What is Mr. Sorensen's attitude in lines 9–10 when he says, "An interesting 'grocery' list, Mister Jackson!"? Do you see a change in the level of formality here?
4. Why do Mr. Sorensen and Richard leave the room?
5. What upset Mr. Sorensen the most?
6. How did Richard respond to Mr. Sorensen's anger?
7. Mr. Sorensen did not hear Richard's last remark. What do you think the result would be if he had?

Dialogue B

Melanie: Hi, Carole!
Carole: Hi, Melanie! This should be a great show. Let's go in.
Melanie: Sure. Say, did you bring my book?
Carole: Your book? Oh, nuts! I completely forgot.
5   Melanie: You forgot!? But you promised! I need it to study for the test. Oh, I knew I never should have loaned it to you.
Carole: Calm down, Melanie. I just forgot. Look, after the show we can drive by the house and pick it up.
Melanie: It's pretty far out of the way, but I guess we'll have to.
10 Carole: Don't worry. I'll treat you to a pizza to make it up to you.
Melanie: Well, OK.

Oh, nuts: expression of dismay
to make something up to someone: to recompense someone; pay them back

Discussion

1. Why is Melanie upset in line 5? (two reasons)
2. How does Carole fix up the argument? Does she apologize?
3. Are the women in the dialogue close friends? How can you tell?

Dialogue C

Mr. Walters:	Hey, can you get your dog to shut up? Some people are trying to sleep around here!
Mrs. Hudson:	Now, wait a minute! Prince is just barking because your cat is screaming all over the place!
Mr. Walters:	But do you know what time it is? It's one a.m., and I've got to get up at six to go to work. If I don't get some sleep soon, there's going to be one less dog in the world.
Mrs. Hudson:	Are you threatening *my* dog?
Mr. Walters:	I am merely telling the truth. Barking at night has been proven to be one of the leading causes of death in dogs.
Mrs. Hudson:	You're nuts!
Mr. Walters:	That's possible. But please, can't you get that mutt to close his trap for a few minutes? Or do you want me to call the cops?
Mrs. Hudson:	You ought to shut your own trap. *You're* the one making the most noise now!
Mr. Walters:	That does it! Bernice! Get the arsenic!
Mrs. Hudson:	(*to the dog*) Come here, Prince. Nice boy. I'm going to take you inside. I don't trust that crazy old man next door. (*to Mr. Walters*) I'M TAKING HIM IN, SO YOU DON'T HAVE TO CALL THE COPS! AND I HOPE YOU SLEEP TILL NEXT YEAR!

you're nuts: you're crazy
mutt: (slang) dog
close his trap: (impolite) close his mouth, be quiet
the cops: (slang) the police

Discussion

1. Who are the two characters in this dialogue, where are they, and what time is it?
2. Why is Mr. Walters angry? How does he express his anger in the first two lines? How does Mrs. Hudson respond? Why do you think she responds this way?
3. What new tactic does Mr. Walters use in lines 6–8? How successful is this tactic?
4. What other tactic does Mr. Walters use in lines 10–12? Is this any more successful?
5. Who is Mrs. Hudson talking to in lines 20–21? lines 22–24?

General discussion

Can you rank the dialogues in order of formality, or do they all seem about the same? Do you find any expressions or intonational patterns that occur in more than one dialogue?

2 EXPRESSING ANGER AND RESOLVING CONFLICT

There are many things that make people angry. Some of these are fairly predictable given the situation. Others are highly personal and idiosyncratic. In this unit, we will outline some of the things that make many Americans angry. You must be cautious when expressing or reacting to anger in a language not your own. If you say the wrong thing, the situation could get worse. It is best to try to resolve the issue.

The following situations will make many Americans angry:

1. *Breaking a promise.* Americans consider their word to be their bond. When someone promises to do something and then does not, that person is considered untrustworthy.
2. *Lying.* There is a fine line between "white lies," such as shaving a few years off one's age, and lies. White lies are not considered harmful, whereas lies – untruths – are seen as the mark of a faulty character. (See Dialogue A.)
3. *Interfering in personal matters.* Americans are taught as children to "mind their own business." People generally do not intrude in other people's personal matters, such as money, sex, and family problems, including the raising of children, religion, and politics.
4. *Breaking a confidence.* When an American tells someone something "between you and me," or "in confidence," or says "I know this won't go any farther," it is expected that no one else will hear the secret. This rule varies widely according to the people involved and the nature of the secret, but it is generally a

good idea not to tell other people things told to you in confidence. (See Unit 5, Dialogue C.)

5. *Taking something without permission.* Generally, Americans are happy to lend their personal property if they are asked. But they do not like it if things are taken without permission.

6. *Being insulting.* There are many types of insults, but the most common are intentional (or unintentional) personal remarks.

7. *Failing to apologize.* If there has been an obvious wrong, such as a child who has gone up and down the street letting air out of all the tires on the cars, people expect an apology (in this case, from the child's parents). If a person fails to apologize, it is a mark against that person's character.

8. *Failing to speak in passing.* It is considered poor manners to "snub" friends, that is, to pass by them on the street without saying hello.

9. *Failing to thank someone.* Failure to express gratitude for a gift or acknowledge a compliment is considered rude behavior.

10. *Failing to return invitations.* A person who has been invited by a friend on several occasions is expected to reciprocate.

Expressing anger

There are several possible ways to express anger or hostility.

1. *Blowing off steam.* Many times, a person who is angry will "blow off steam" by voicing anger to the nearest sympathetic listener, rather than the person he or she is angry with. The listener tries to console the angry person *by agreeing with his or her anger* or by trying to play peacemaker and resolve the conflict.

2. *Mild rebuke.* Perhaps the most difficult way of expressing anger, this is the most acceptable of those strategies outlined here. A person who makes a mild rebuke states what is making him or her angry and suggests a way of solving the problem. (See Dialogue B.)

3. *Extreme politeness.* This is an acceptable way of making anger clear. In this situation, the angry person suddenly becomes extremely polite, using either the *title + last name* or *full name* form to address the listener, thus psychologically distancing himself or herself from the listener. Usually, the angry person talks slower and more distinctly, and uses a lower voice than normal. (See Dialogue A.)

4. *Silence.* The angry person uses non-verbal (without words) gestures to show emotion, such as an icy stare. Some people do not like this method, however, since they believe that people should talk about their problems. Some people will even get mad if they are given "the silent treatment."

5. *Sarcasm.* This technique involves using nice words in a very unnice way. Usually, it is the intonation that makes the difference. A false smile may also accompany the words. Many people consider sarcasm offensive, expecially when used very often. (See Dialogue A.)

6. *Screaming and yelling.* In this strategy, the idea is to talk loud and fast, mixing in as many swear words as possible. Door slamming may be used to punctuate the sentences. This type of behavior, although widespread, is not considered appropriate. A person using this method is considered to be "out of control" or "acting like a child." (See Dialogue C.)
7. *Threatening.* This usually happens after an initial period of screaming and yelling. This is also not considered appropriate. (See Dialogue C.)

Resolving conflict

When there is a conflict, the best thing to do is to try to resolve it so that relationships remain good. Some people avoid discussing a conflict. Others become angry themselves. Neither reaction to anger is very useful in settling a dispute. Here are three ways to resolve a conflict:

1. *Apologize.* This involves accepting responsibility for the offense (see Unit 5). An apology is often the best response to an expression of anger and, if sincere, will help to calm the other person down. An apology may have to be repeated before the other person will accept it (see Dialogue B).
2. *Offer to discuss the matter.* If someone is angry with you, but you don't know why, the best thing to do is ask: "I'm sorry you're angry, but I don't understand why. Please, let's discuss it calmly."
3. *Find a mediator.* If you "blow off steam" to a friend, you can sometimes get advice on how to settle a conflict or can possibly get your friend to intercede with the person who is angry. He or she can discuss the dispute and then get the two of you together again.

OFFER TO DISCUSS THE MATTER.

Taboo words

In all languages there are words that are considered "bad" to use. They should be avoided, because they are offensive to most people. Besides, there are other expressions you can use to express your anger or frustration.

Discussion

How do you usually express anger? What are common ways in your country for showing anger or frustration? Are there gestures that you use? Are there things that Americans do that upset or anger you? How can you deal with that anger?

---

3 PHRASES 📼

Directions: Listen to the following phrases on the tape as you read along here. Then practice saying them. The phrases near the top of the list are generally more formal than the ones near the bottom.

BLOWING OFF STEAM	RESPONSE
It annoys me when...	I don't like it either.
I don't like it when...	I don't like it either.
I can't stand it when...	I know what you mean.
It burns me up when...	Me, too.
I hate it when...	So do I.

	RESOLVING CONFLICT	RESPONSE
More formal	I'd like to discuss this matter.	That would be a good idea.
	Can we discuss this?	
↕	Please, let's discuss this.	Yes, let's.
Less formal	Don't be angry. Let's talk it over.	
	Come on. Don't be mad.	

4 SMALL GROUP PRACTICE

A. Using what you've learned

Directions: For each situation that follows, read the cues given, then discuss the relationship among the speakers and the level of formality. Using this information, complete the dialogues orally with phrases from Section 3 or with any other appropriate response. Example:

A: Hello?

B: *Hi, Bob. Can you help me out?*

A: Do you know what time it is?

B: *I know it's late. I'm sorry.*

A: *OK. What can I do?*

Situation 1

A: Would you please be quiet! I'm trying to _____.
B:
A: I'm sorry, but I'm just nervous about finishing.
B:

Situation 2

A:
B: What do you want *now*?
A:
B:

Situation 3

A:
B: Fine, thanks.
A:
B: I think you should mind your own business!
A:

Situation 4

A: Hey, where were you last night? We waited an *hour* for you!
B:
A:

B. Cued dialogues

Directions: After looking at each situation carefully, discuss with your partner the relationship among the speakers and the appropriate level of formality. Then practice, using any words or expressions appropriate to express the functions given. Your teacher will ask you to perform the dialogue for the class.

Situation 1

X and Y are friends. But X had a big party last weekend and didn't invite Y, even though Y always invites X to Y's parties. Y sees that X is just getting home from work and goes over to talk.

Y	X
1. greets X	1. greets Y
2. asks how the party was	2. answers question
3. expresses anger	3. apologizes, explains why Y wasn't invited
4. expresses disappointment	4. repeats apology
5. accepts apology	5. invites Y
6. accepts invitation, expresses pleasure	6. expresses pleasure
7. gives preclosing	7. responds to preclosing
8. says good-bye	8. says good-bye

Situation 2

B has just come to town to go to the university and needs to find an apartment. B is talking with a classmate, A, before class on the first day of school.

A	B
1. introduces self	1. introduces self, asks about A's home
2. gives information, asks where B is living now	2. answers question, asks about housing in the area
3. gives general information	3. asks about rents
4. gives information	4. asks about A's rent
5. expresses anger	5. apologizes and gives excuse
6. accepts apology	6. asks A to go along to the housing office
7. agrees to do this	7. expresses thanks
8. acknowledges thanks	

C. Mini-roleplays

Directions: Discuss the situation with your partner and decide on the proper level of formality. You can use the suggested expressions if you want to. Then practice. When you are ready, perform for the class and discuss your performance with your teacher and classmates.

Roleplay 1

A promised B to fix B's bicycle by Friday so B could go on a week-end bike trip with some friends. However, A got tickets to the ball-game at the last minute, so A didn't have time to fix the bike. Act out the scene where A explains to B why the bicycle isn't fixed.

Useful expressions

A	B
opportunity to see Reggie Jackson	trip of a lifetime training for weeks

Roleplay 2

A and B share an office in a publishing firm. A has a very nice set of pencils for making illustrations. One day when A is on a coffee break, B breaks a pencil. B finds one in A's set and is using it when A returns. A sees the pencil and the open set, and is very angry.

Useful expressions

A	B
no privacy around here can't leave anything unlocked	broke my own pencil only borrowing it

7 Giving compliments and replying to compliments

In this unit, we will look at situations that require a compliment and practice giving compliments. These situations may be different from those requiring compliments in your native culture. You will also learn what to say when you want to give a compliment to someone in English.

As you listen to the dialogues, listen especially for the compliments you hear, and note what the person is complimenting. Also pay attention to how the other person replies to the compliment.

1   DIALOGUES 📼

Dialogue A

Cal: Hey, man, how you doing?
RC: Not too bad. How about you? What's this machine you're leaning on? Somebody pay you to look after his wheels?
Cal: No. It's mine. Mine and the bank's.
5 RC: (*whistles*) She's a beauty! How she drive?
Cal: Like a dream. Even on the potholes around here.
RC: That's great, man. Maybe you'll let me borrow her sometime.
Cal: Glad you like it, but my own mother doesn't get to use it. Anybody dents it, it's going to be me.
10 RC: Yeah, I can understand that. I'd do the same if I had a machine like this. Well, see you around.
Cal: So long.

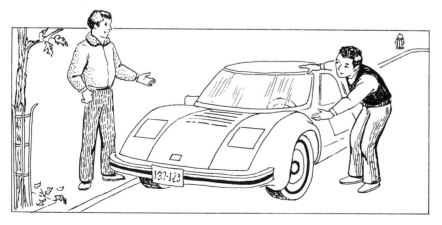

man: (slang) can refer to a man or a woman

wheels: (slang) car

pothole: hole in the pavement on a street caused by freezing and
thawing

Discussion

1. How many different ways does RC compliment Cal on his car?
2. How does Cal acknowledge the compliment?

Dialogue B

	(The doorbell rings.)
George Burns:	Hi! Come in!
Jack Palmer:	Hi, George. Thank you.
Mary Palmer:	Hello, George. How are you?
George Burns:	Just fine, thanks, Mary. And you?
Mary Palmer:	Fine.
Donna Burns:	*(coming to greet them)* Sorry, last-minute things in the oven.
Jack:	These are for you.
Donna:	Oh, thank you! They're beautiful!
Mary:	What a lovely home you have!
Donna:	Why, thank you. I'm so glad you could come. Let's sit here so we can see the garden as the sun goes down.
Mary:	Your garden is beautiful, Donna.
Donna:	Thank you.
Mary:	What are those tall flowers in the back?
Donna:	Those are salvias. Would you like some?
Mary:	Thanks so much, but I don't have a spot of sun to grow them in.
Donna:	That's right. George mentioned that you and Jack are specialists in shade flowers. Aren't you two illustrating a book? That must be very interesting.
Mary:	It's nice of you to remember. Yes, we're doing a book for the Wildlife Federation.
Donna:	Well, I've got this one shady corner that I have trouble with. Maybe you can give me some advice.
Mary:	I'll try.
Donna:	We'll just have time for a look before dinner. Back in a minute, dear.
George:	OK. Jack and I will admire the view from here.

Discussion

1. What gift does Jack Palmer give Donna Burns? How does she react?
2. Find the exchanges of compliments and their responses. Note especially the way Donna compliments Mary.

2 GIVING AND RESPONDING TO COMPLIMENTS

Purpose

Compliments express approval, and their main purpose is to show that you like some aspect of the other person's appearance, belongings, or work. This reassures the other person that his or her taste, appearance, etc., is appreciated by other people.

Some people use compliments to "butter up" somebody, or to flatter in order to increase goodwill. Therefore, overuse of compliments might seem insincere.

Whom to compliment

You may compliment anyone you have occasion to talk with. It may be a close friend or someone you have just met. And in certain cases you can compliment a stranger in order to get some information:

You: Excuse me, but I was just admiring your bag. It's really nice.
Stranger: Oh, thank you.
You: Would you mind telling me where you got it? I've been looking for one like that for a long time.
Stranger: It's from that luggage store down on York Avenue.
You: Oh, thank you very much.

What to compliment

Usually, you compliment someone if you notice something new about the person's appearance: new eyeglasses, a new haircut, an article of clothing, or a piece of jewelry. You may also compliment a person on his or her general appearance: "Gee, you really look good today" or "You're looking trim these days." It is customary to compliment a person on a recently purchased item: "Hey, I really like your new car" or "That new dress is a gorgeous shade of blue."

When you visit someone's house for the first time, you can give a general compliment, such as "What a beautiful house you have." Or if you know the house and you notice some new furniture or a redecorated room, you can compliment the person on the new items.

When hosts prepare a meal for you, or even just snack food at a party, they like to hear that you appreciate the food. You do not need to compliment each dish separately, but you can give a general compliment, followed by a specific one: "The meal was delicious, especially the lamb."

In many cultures it is considered inappropriate to compliment babies, but in the U.S. it is common: "What a cute baby!"

How to compliment

There are three ways to give a compliment: by saying something nice about the object, by asking how the person made it or where it was bought (but *not* how much it cost), or by asking for another look or another serving, if it is food.

Replying to compliments

There are two basic ways of replying to compliments: accepting them and rejecting them. In most cases, it is best to *accept* the compliment. To do this, you can either thank the person and explain something about the thing being complimented, or you can return the compliment by giving the other person a similar compliment. When accepting the compliment, the dialogue might go like this:

Al: That's a beautiful dress you have on!
Gay: Oh, thank you. I just got it yesterday.

When returning the compliment, it might go like this:

Alice: I just love your hair that way! Did you do it yourself?
Juanita: Oh, thanks. Yes, I did. Isn't yours a new cut, too?
Alice: Yes, it is. Thanks.

In certain cases, you may accept the compliment but deny what the person has said to compliment you. Some people do this to appear modest:

1. Friend: That was a great dinner. You must have spent all day cooking.
   You: Thanks. But it really only took an hour.

2. Friend: Wow, this is really a nice place!
   You: Aw, thanks, but it's really nothing great.

Discussion

How do you react to compliments? Do people in your country compliment babies? Are you complimented on your wife's or husband's success? Is it appropriate in your culture to compliment the food? a woman's dress?

3 PHRASES 🔲

Directions: Listen to the following phrases on the tape as you read along here. Then practice saying them. The phrases near the top of the list are generally more formal than the ones near the bottom.

	COMPLIMENT	RESPONSE	RETURNING COMPLIMENT (OPTIONAL)
More formal	I would like to compliment you on . . .	Thank you. It's nice of you to say so.	(You inspired me.)
	I would like to compliment you on . . .		It's nice to hear that from someone with your experience.
	I think your (hair) is very nice.	Thank you, but it really isn't anything special.	
	I just love your . . .	Thank you. Yours is even nicer.	
	The (chicken) is delicious.	I'm glad you like it.	
	I really like your . . . !	Thank you.	Yours is nice, too.
	This (cheese) is super.		
	That's not a bad (bike) you've got.		
	That's neat.		
	That's nice.		
	That's not bad.		
	Terrific.	Thanks.	
	Pretty good.		
Less formal	OK!		
	All right.		

Note: It is sometimes sufficient simply to say "Thank you" to a compliment. No further reply is required.

4 SMALL GROUP PRACTICE

A. Using what you've learned

Directions: For each situation that follows, read the cues given, then discuss the relationship among the speakers and the level of formality. Using this information, complete the dialogues orally with phrases from Section 3 or with any other appropriate responses. Example:

A: That's a great sweater!

B: Why, thank you. I just bought it yesterday.

Situation 1

A: Hi, Joe. Hey, is that a new _____?
B:
A:
B:

Situation 2

A: Well, thank you for the _____.
B:
A: Yes, I really _____.
B:

Situation 3

A:
B: Oh, thanks. I just lost five pounds.
A:
B:

Situation 4

A: Good morning, Jones.
B:
A:
B: Well, thank you, Mr. Tweed. But I was just doing my job.
A: Yes, and we're proud of you, Jones.
B:

B. Cued dialogues

Directions: After looking at each situation carefully, discuss with your partner the relationship among the speakers and the appropriate level of formality. Then practice, using any words or expressions appropriate to express the functions given. Your teacher will ask you to perform the dialogue for the class.

Situation 1

A works in an office where *X* is the supervisor. *X* has invited everyone from the office to a cocktail party one evening. There *A* talks with *B*, *X*'s spouse.

B	*A*
1. greets *A*	1. greets *B*, compliments *B* on clothing
2. accepts compliment, returns compliment	2. accepts compliment
3. offers food	3. accepts, compliments *B* on the food
4. refuses compliment, gives preclosing	4. replies to preclosing
5. tells *A* to have a good time	5. agrees to

Situation 2

A and *B* are good friends from school. *A* sees *B* on a new motorcycle and begins to talk with *B*.

A	*B*
1. greets *B*	1. returns greeting
2. compliments *B* on new motorcycle	2. accepts compliment, tells when motorcycle was bought
3. asks to try motorcycle	3. agrees *or* refuses and gives reason
4. expresses thanks *or* expresses disappointment	

C. Mini-roleplays

Directions: Discuss the situation with your partner and decide on the proper level of formality. You can use the suggested expressions if you want to. Then practice. When you are ready, perform for the class and discuss your performance with your teacher and classmates.

Roleplay 1

A has just eaten dinner at *B*'s apartment. *A* really liked the meal, except for the dessert, which *A* couldn't finish. They are leaving the dinner table, and *A* feels obliged to say something about the meal to *B*.

Useful expressions

A	*B*
dessert – very rich	typical meal
chicken – delicious	love to cook
must have taken hours	not hard at all

Roleplay 2

A has been invited to *B*'s home for dinner. It is the first time *A* has been there, and *B* is showing *A* around the house.

Useful expressions

A	*B*
comfortable	family room
interesting painting	local artist

Roleplay 3

A is showing pictures of *A*'s newborn baby to *B*, a co-worker at the factory. *A* has several pictures and is very proud of the baby.

Useful expressions

A	*B*
football player	big baby
	cute

Roleplay 4

A, an executive in a large company, has lost a lot of weight recently by avoiding alcohol and exercising regularly. *A* happens to meet *B*, an old friend. They haven't seen each other in quite a while.

Useful expressions

A	*B*
kick the habit	look terrific

8 Getting people's attention and interrupting

There are certain occasions when you must interrupt people who are in the middle of doing something else. It is important to know *how* to do this, as well as *when* it is socially acceptable to do it. In this lesson, you will study interrupting people and getting people's attention, two functions that are very closely linked.

Listen to the following dialogues, listening in particular to how people get other people's attention, and when and how they interrupt each other. Note also how people react to the interruptions.

1 DIALOGUES 📼

Dialogue A

(Freddy stops at Dr. Lindseth's open office door and knocks.)

Freddy: Dr. Lindseth?

Dr. Lindseth: Yes?

Freddy: Excuse me, I don't want to interrupt you...

Dr. Lindseth: No, no. It's quite all right. How can I help you?

5 Freddy: Well, I'd just like to ask you to sign a permission slip to take that course on microbiology you're teaching next term. Would that be all right? *(He gives Dr. Lindseth the slip.)*

Dr. Lindseth: Of course, Freddy. Actually, I'm glad you decided to
10 take it. I think you'll like it, and I'm glad to have you in the class.

Freddy: Thank you. It sounds like an interesting course.

Dr. Lindseth: I'm glad you think so. *(She signs the slip.)* There you are. *(She gives the paper back to Freddy.)*

15 Freddy: Thank you very much. Good-bye, Dr. Lindseth.

Dr. Lindseth: Good-bye, Freddy.

Discussion

1. How does Freddy get Dr. Lindseth's attention? (2 ways)
2. What function is Freddy performing in line 3?
3. Why does Freddy thank Dr. Lindseth in line 12?
4. What function does Freddy express in line 12?
5. Paraphrase the expression, "There you are" (lines 13–14).
6. What is Freddy thanking Dr. Lindseth for in line 15?
7. How formal is this conversation?

Dialogue B

Jean: ... and then *she* told me that *he* didn't even say he was *sorry!*
Sue: No kidding.
Max: Excuse me, but could I ask you a quick question?
Sue: Sure. What is it?
Max: Do you spell "address" with one "d" or two?
Sue: Two.
Max: Thanks a lot.
Sue: Sure. (*to Jean*) *Then* what did she say?

Discussion

1. Who are the speakers and what are they doing?
2. How does Max interrupt? What is the reaction?
3. Why does Max interrupt?
4. Paraphrase Sue's response to Max in line 8.
5. How formal is this conversation?

Dialogue C

	(*The telephone rings.*)
JoEllen:	Linguistics.
Ralph:	Yes, I'd like to speak with Dr. MacDougal, please.
JoEllen:	Who's calling, please?
Ralph:	Ralph Zimmermann.
5 JoEllen:	One moment, please. (*buzz*)
Dr. MacDougal:	Yes?
JoEllen:	Excuse me, there's a Ralph Zimmermann on the line. Do you want to talk to him?
Dr. MacDougal:	No, have him call back later. I'll be in a meeting now until twelve o'clock. Would you please hold my calls?
JoEllen:	Of course, Dr. MacDougal. (*click*) I'm sorry, sir, but Dr. MacDougal is in a meeting right now. Would you like to leave a message?
15 Ralph:	Could you tell me what time he'll be free?
JoEllen:	Well, the meeting's scheduled to last till twelve. Would you like to call back then?
Ralph:	Oh, I'm afraid I can't. Could you ask him to call me this afternoon at home?
20 JoEllen:	Your number?
Ralph:	512-8946. Thank you very much.
JoEllen:	You're welcome.

Discussion

1. Who are the speakers, and what are their relationships?
2. Why doesn't Dr. MacDougal want to talk with Ralph at this time? (This is one situation in which an interruption is not tolerated except in an emergency.)
3. Who apologizes in this dialogue, and why?
4. What function does JoEllen serve for Dr. MacDougal?
5. Do you think this is a formal situation?

2 GETTING PEOPLE'S ATTENTION AND INTERRUPTING

Getting people's attention and interrupting people are important skills in any language. These are sometimes difficult to do in another culture, where the gestures or ways of speaking are very different from your own. As always, the formality of the situation and the relationship of the speakers will affect the way people talk to each other.

Getting people's attention

In general, it is most polite to be as unobtrusive as possible when trying to get someone's attention. In most situations it is best to wait until the other person is looking in your direction and then try to "catch his eye." However, that does not always work. Here are some other ways.

In a restaurant or store

As the waiter or waitress is going by, raise your hand, palm out, and say "Waiter" or "Miss" in a voice just loud enough to carry above the restaurant noise. Customers in restaurants do not snap their fingers.

In a store, if the salesperson is visible, but is not looking at you, you can say, "Excuse me."

In class

To ask a question in class, you can raise your hand and wait to be acknowledged. If the professor does not look up often, raise your hand and call the professor's name using the *title* + *last name* form. It is not customary to snap one's fingers or to address the professor as "Teacher."

On the street

Unless you can catch the person's eye with a wave, it is better not to try to get someone's attention on the street. Shouting and whistling attract too much attention and are considered rude.

In an office

In general, if someone is at work, but not in private conference, his or her office door is open. To get that person's attention, knock on the door and wait to be acknowledged. Do not enter the office until given permission to do so. If the door is shut, you may be interrupting something by knocking, so follow the guidelines in the next section.

Interrupting people

Most people do not mind interruptions if they are short ones. Dialogue B, for example, shows Max interrupting a conversation with a quick question. The following is another example of a brief interruption:

Jackie: (*on the phone*) He walks up to me and... Just a minute.
(*to Ted in the office*) Can I help you?
Ted: Excuse me, Jackie, but can I ask a question?
Jackie: Sure.
Ted: Has Dr. Betts sent that letter out, do you know?
Jackie: I think so. She sent a bunch of letters out this morning.
Ted: OK. Thanks.
Jackie: (*on the phone*) Now, as I was saying, this guy walks up to me last night and says...

If the interruption is not a quick one, and if it is not an emergency, there is something you can do. You can ask to make an appointment with the person.

Mr. Andrews: (*talking to a salesperson*)... which means that the ratio will be all wrong. Excuse me. Yes?
Mr. Davidson: (*standing in the doorway*) Excuse me for interrupting, but could we make an appointment for later this afternoon sometime? I want to go over that engineering report with you.

Other interruptions

Calling on the telephone is sometimes an interruption. If you call someone at dinnertime or late in the evening (after ten o'clock), you should first ask if it is a good time to talk. If not, you can arrange to call back later.

Joe: Hello?
Ned: Hi, this is Ned. Are you busy?
Joe: We're eating now. Can I call back in half an hour?
Ned: OK. See you.
Joe: Yeah, bye.

In conversation it is considered impolite to interrupt in the middle of a sentence – you should wait until the sentence has been completed. This is called "turn taking" and helps minimize the confusion that comes from not listening to what the other person is saying.

Interrupting strangers is normally not done, since it is not considered polite to "eavesdrop," or listen in on someone else's conversation. However, it sometimes happens on occasions when someone is being helpful. In an elevator, for example, if you hear people discussing which floor they should get off on and they have the wrong one, you can interrupt to give them the correct information (see the phrases in Section 3).

Discussion

Is whistling at someone considered an appropriate way of getting their attention in your country? Are there gestures you use to attract people's attention? When is it all right to interrupt? How do people react to interruptions?

3 PHRASES 🔲

Directions: Listen to the following phrases on the tape as you read
along here. Then practice saying them. The phrases near the top of
the list are generally more formal than the ones near the bottom.

	GETTING SOMEONE'S ATTENTION	RESPONSE
More formal	Pardon me, Dr. Nathanson.	Yes? What can I do for you?
	Excuse me, Bill.	
↑	Oh, Miss?	Yes? (Can I help you?)
	Sir?	
⏐	Waiter?	
↓	(cough)	Yes?
Less formal	(clear throat)	Yes?
	Hey, Beth.	Yeah?
Rude	Hey you!	(In most cases one would
	Hey!	receive no response or a ruder
	(Whistle)	one.)

	INTERRUPTING A CONVERSATION	RESPONSE
More formal	Pardon me, but...	How can I help?
	Pardon the interruption, but...	
↑	I'm sorry to interrupt you, but...	
	I don't want to interrupt you, but...	It's all right. What can I do for you?
⏐	I hate to interrupt, but...	
	I'm sorry, but...	It's OK.
↓	Excuse me, but...	
Less formal	Oh, were you in the middle of something?	No. It's all right.
	Am I interrupting?	

	INTERRUPTING AN OVERHEARD CONVERSATION	RESPONSE
More formal	Excuse me, but (I think you want the eighteenth floor, not the twenty-eighth).	Oh. Thanks.
↑	I'd like to say something, if you don't mind.	Go ahead.
⏐	It's none of my business, but...	
↓	Do you mind if I say something?	
Less formal	Can I butt in here?	Sure.
	Excuse me, but...	

4 SMALL GROUP PRACTICE

A. Using what you've learned

Directions: For each situation that follows, read the cues given, then discuss the relationship among the speakers and the level of formality. Using this information, complete the dialogues orally with phrases from Section 3 or with any other appropriate response. Example:

A: *Those are great boots.*

B: Why, thank you. I got them yesterday on sale.

C: Excuse me, but *do you have the time?*

A: *Nine thirty-five.*

C: *Thanks.*

A: You're welcome.

Situation 1

A: What happened next?
B: Well, I started down the dark alley . . .
C:
B:
C: Do you have change for a ten?
A:
C:
B: As I was saying. . .

Situation 2

A: . . . so I think parents should not allow children to watch TV at all!
B: Well, I'm not sure if I agree. I think _____.
C: _____, but I overheard you talking about _____. Can I say something?
A:
C:
B:
C:

Situation 3

A: ... So I guess I'll be seeing you later.
B:
C: _____. Have you got a minute? I _____.
A:
C:
A:
C: _____. That helps a lot.

B. Cued dialogues

Directions: After looking at each situation carefully, discuss with your partner(s) the relationship among the speakers and the appropriate level of formality. Then practice, using any words or expressions appropriate to express the functions given. Your teacher will ask you to perform the dialogue for the class.

Situation 1

A is a student in a technical program, and *B* is *A*'s adviser. *A* goes to see *B* in *B*'s office. When *A* gets there, *B* is talking on the phone.

B	*A*
1. excuses self (to caller), greets *A*	1. greets *B*, apologizes for interrupting
2. accepts apology, closes the phone conversation	2. asks for appointment
3. suggests a time	3. rejects the time
4. suggests another time	4. accepts the time, thanks *B*
5. replies to thanks	5. gives closing
6. replies to closing	

Situation 2

A is waiting for the elevator in a large department store, but the elevator doesn't come. *A* is about to give up but suddenly hears people screaming in the elevator shaft. *A* decides that they must be stuck in the elevator between floors. *A* runs to the nearest cashier, where there is a telephone. *B* and *C*, who are working there, are talking when *A* comes over.

B	C	A
1. compliments C on her skirt	1. replies to compliment, returns the compliment	
2. replies to compliment		2. gets B's attention
3. asks A to wait		3. interrupts and gives reason, asks B to call for help
4. makes a phone call	4. expresses concern	4. explains what happened
5. gives the result of the phone call		

Situation 3

A is walking down the street in a new city, looking for Dawson Street. *A* sees two people talking together on the street and tries to catch their eye to ask for directions.

B	C	A
1. invites C to a beer party	1. asks for more information	
2. gives information	2. accepts invitation, offers to bring something	
3. accepts offer, tells C what to bring	3. agrees, expresses pleasure	
4. offers to help stranger		4. apologizes for interrupting, asks for Dawson St.
5. expresses ignorance	5. asks what the house number is	5. gives the number
	6. tells A location	6. thanks C for help, gives parting
	7. returns parting	

C. Mini-roleplays

Directions: Discuss the situation with your partner(s) and decide on the proper level of formality. You can use the suggested expressions if you want to. Then practice. When you are ready, perform for the class and discuss your performance with your teacher and classmates.

Roleplay 1

Professor *A* is working quietly in the office on a report that is taking all day to complete. *B*, a student, drops by to talk about a research paper that is due in two days.

Useful expressions

A	*B*
deadline for a report	extension of the deadline
put things off till the last minute	final draft
learning self-discipline	two other reports due

Roleplay 2

A is sitting in the library trying to finish reading a book before a final exam begins in half an hour. First, *B* comes by to say hi, then *C* wants the answer to a geometry question, and then *D* needs change for a twenty-dollar bill. *A* is polite in the beginning, but quickly loses patience as time runs out.

Useful expressions

A	*B*	*C*	*D*
study for a test	haven't seen you for a while	formula for the area of a circle	a ten and two fives
terrible at math	what's new?		

Roleplay 3

A is having lunch with a friend, *B*. *A* must be back at the office in an hour. The restaurant is not crowded, but the service is slow because the waiter stops to chat with other customers. *A* tries to get the waiter's attention to order. When the food finally arrives it is cold, and *A* has to call the waiter again to point this out.

Useful expressions

A AND B	*WAITER*
a one o'clock meeting	I'll be right there.
an appointment	Just one moment.

9 Agreeing and disagreeing

In talking about almost anything, and especially when discussing certain topics, such as religion, sports, the economy, or politics, you hear many opinions expressed. You will probably agree with some and disagree with others. This section describes appropriate ways of doing this in English.

Listen to the dialogues, paying careful attention to the opinions that are expressed, and the way people *agree* and *disagree* with those opinions.

1 DIALOGUES 🔲

Dialogue A

Ned: ... you know, I think this country's problems all come from inflation. *That's* the main cause of our troubles right now. And what's causing the inflation? It's the reckless spending of the Democrats! Every year, they spend more
5 and more money, and that money has to come from somewhere. So we pay it in the form of higher taxes and higher prices on the goods we buy.

Barbara: Well, I'm not sure that I agree with you. It seems to me that inflation is only one of our problems. What about
10 unemployment? If people don't have jobs because the government cuts spending too much, they can't buy things; and then you have a vicious circle of more unemployment and fewer taxpayers to share the burden.

Ellen: You know, I think Barb may have something there. Unem-
15 ployment *is* a big problem, especially in the big industrial cities. The auto industry is fighting for its life right now, and the government isn't doing very much to help it.

Ned: Well, it's true that the auto industry *is* in a mess, but I don't think the answer is in government regulation or pro-
20 tection. I believe in the free market system – let the system work without a lot of government interference, and everything will be OK.

Ellen: So the strong will win, and the weak will be defeated. Is that what you mean?

25   Ned: Well, that's the way it goes. The survival of the fittest.

Barbara: And too bad about the weak, the poor, the unprotected...

Ned: Now you're getting emotional. You have to remain objective about these things. Let me give you an example of what I'm talking about...

Discussion

1. What is the subject of the discussion?
2. Does everyone agree on what the problem is?
3. In the first 22 lines, there are two examples of one person agreeing with another's opinion, and two examples of one person disagreeing with another. Find the two examples of each function. What words do they use to show agreement? How do they express disagreement?
4. What is the level of formality? Does this seem to be a fight or a friendly argument?

Dialogue B

Jean: ... so she said they're moving to Corvallis in the fall, because Jeffrey got a job at the university.

Dotty: Oh, where's that? Isn't that in California, or someplace?

Lisa: No, that's in Idaho, a little north of Boise, I think. I have a
5   cousin there.

Jean: But I thought it was in Oregon. At least, that was the impression I got from Nancy. She said it wouldn't be far to Portland.

Lisa: Oh, you're right. I guess I was thinking of something else. Forget what I said.

Discussion

1. What is the subject of the dispute?
2. Who is moving to Corvallis?
3. There are two instances of disagreement here and one instance of agreement. What words does each woman use to express her agreement or disagreement?
4. What inference can you make about the level of formality?

Dialogue C

David: ... and *he* said he bought his new car for five thousand!
Mary Alice: What kind is it?
David: A BMW – I'm not sure what model.
Mary Alice: Are you sure? A BMW for five thousand? Sounds pretty
5   cheap to me!
David: Well, I think that's what he said.
Mary Alice: But they don't make a model for less than eight or nine
              thousand!
David: Well, you'll have to ask him. Come to think of it, it *does*
10   sound awful cheap...

Discussion

1. What are the speakers discussing?
2. Who bought the car?
3. How does Mary Alice indicate her doubt? What line is that in?
4. What function is Mary Alice expressing in lines 8–9?
5. How does David react when his information is challenged? How
   does his confidence change from the first to the last lines?
6. How formal is this dialogue?

2 AGREEING AND DISAGREEING

Agreeing with someone

It is easy to agree with someone, on any level of formality: "I agree completely with what you said in your lecture" or "Yeah, that's right, Dave." The only way to get into trouble is by being insincere and only pretending to agree. A person who always agrees with someone else and never has an individual opinion is not respected. This is especially true in employer–employee relationships. If the employee always agrees with the boss, the employee is called a "Yes-man." It is OK to disagree with superiors, as long as it is done in an acceptable way.

Disagreeing with someone

There are two ways to disagree with someone: directly and indirectly.

Direct
Mary: The show finishes at ten o'clock.
Chuck: No, it doesn't. They told me eleven.

When you disagree directly you should be sure of your facts, because being wrong will require an apology. Notice the appeal to "higher authority" ("*They* told me...").

Indirect
Mary: The show finishes at ten o'clock.
Chuck: Oh, really? That's strange. They told me it would be around eleven.

First Chuck expresses surprise ("Oh, really?"), then doubt ("That's strange"), then gives the facts. As long as it is factual information that is in dispute, either form of disagreeing is acceptable, although indirect disagreement often sounds more polite.

If you are questioning someone's opinion or judgment, it is better to use indirect techniques, such as:

1. turning a statement into a question: "Are you sure ...?"
2. agreeing with part of the other person's idea: "I agree that X, but Y..."
3. using introductory remarks: "I could be wrong, but..."

Look back at the dialogues to find examples of these.

Discussion

How can you express disagreement in your culture? Do you usually use direct or indirect methods? Do employees in your country disagree openly with their superiors?

3 PHRASES 📼

Directions: Listen to the following phrases on the tape as you read along here. Then practice saying them. The phrases near the top of the list are generally more formal than the ones near the bottom. Starred (*) phrases are very strong and often impolite.

COMPLETE AGREEMENT

More
formal
  ↕
Less
formal

I agree completely. .
That's just what I think, of course.
In my opinion, you are correct.
I couldn't agree more.
You're right.
Sure.

TENTATIVE AGREEMENT

I suppose you're right.
Well, maybe. . .

INDIRECT DISAGREEMENT

I'm not sure I can agree.
I wonder if there's a mistake.
In my opinion,. . .
Are you absolutely sure?
That really surprises me.
I may be wrong, but. . .
But I thought. . .
Really?
Oh, I don't know.
Yes, but. . .

DIRECT DISAGREEMENT

More
formal
  ↑
  ↓
Less
formal

I'm sorry, but I have to disagree.
I couldn't agree less.
I couldn't disagree more.
I refuse to believe that. . .*
No, that's wrong.*
You're dead wrong.*
Nope.*
No way!*
Uh-uh!*

4 SMALL GROUP PRACTICE

A. Using what you've learned

Directions: For each situation that follows, read the cues given, then discuss the relationship among the speakers and the level of formality. Using this information, complete the dialogues orally with phrases from Section 3 or with any other appropriate response. Example:

A: . . . so then my cousins moved to Milwaukee.

B: Oh, that's in Minnesota, isn't it?

A: *No, it's in Wisconsin.*

B: *Oh, sorry.*

Situation 1

A:

B: I wonder if you heard that wrong. Did he really say that?

A:

B:

A: Well, all I know is what he said to me.

Situation 2

A: Did you know that _____?

B: Are you sure?

A:

B: Well, maybe I'm wrong, but _____.

Situation 3

A: Well, in my opinion, _____.

B: Why do you say that?

A:

B: That's an interesting thought, but _____.

A:

Situation 4

A: What did you think of (the movie)?

B:

A: Oh, I don't know. _____.

B:

A:

B. Cued dialogues

Directions: After looking at each situation carefully, discuss with your partner the relationship among the speakers and the appropriate level of formality. Then practice, using any words or expressions appropriate to express the functions given. Your teacher will ask you to perform the dialogue for the class.

Situation 1

A and *B* are both graduate students in the same class. *A* is sitting in the cafeteria one day and sees *B* carrying a tray...

A	B
1. greets *B*	1. greets *A*
2. asks *B* how the test went yesterday	2. answers question, asks *A* the same question
3. tells *B* his or her test score, asks how *B* studies	3. describes his or her study corner
4. asks for more details	4. gives more information
5. disagrees with *B*'s method, gives own method	5. disagrees with *A*'s method, asks what is the most important thing for studying
6. gives opinion	6. expresses doubt, gives own opinion
7. gives tentative agreement, gives preclosing	7. replies to preclosing
8. says good-bye	8. says good-bye

Situation 2

A and *B* are neighbors. They meet on the street and begin to talk about nuclear energy.

A	B
1. greets *B*	1. greets *A*, asks about *A*'s family
2. says son, Randy, is working in a nuclear plant	2. asks what he will be doing
3. describes Randy's position	3. expresses surprise, introduces the subject of nuclear energy and its dangers
4. agrees that it is a problem, suggests a solution	4. disagrees politely with *A*'s opinion, gives own opinion
5. expresses doubt, asks for more information/explanation	5. gives further explanation/more information
6. gives tentative agreement	6. gives preclosing
7. replies to preclosing	7. says good-bye
8. says good-bye	

C. Mini-roleplays

Directions: Discuss the situation with your partner(s) and decide on the proper level of formality. You can use the suggested expressions if you want to. Then practice. When you are ready, perform for the class and discuss your performance with your teacher and classmates.

Roleplay 1

A and *B* are roommates at school, and they are interested in buying a washing machine for their apartment. *A* wants to buy a new washer, so they'll be sure to have no problems with the machine. *B*, on the other hand, thinks it would be better to buy a used machine, since they only need it for a year or so.

Useful expressions

A	*B*
be sure not to get a lemon	short-term investment
service calls	economical
new washer has warranty	second-hand

lemon: (slang) a poor-quality machine or appliance

Roleplay 2

A, *B*, and *C*, all psychology students, are discussing the best way to raise children. *A* is in favor of a strict, authoritarian upbringing, whereas *C* favors a permissive, relaxed method. *B* prefers to combine both perspectives, depending on the situation.

Useful expressions

A	*B*	*C*
firm discipline	firm but kind guidance	child's rights
spare the rod and spoil the child	teach self-control	can't confuse the child by acting unpredictably
must be consistent	balance is needed	

Roleplay 3

A has been invited by *B* to a dinner party this weekend. *A* accepted the invitation, although *A* doesn't know *B* very well. Now another friend, *C*, wants *A* to come to a party at *C*'s house. *A* prefers the second invitation. *A* is talking to another friend, *D*, about deciding to go to *C*'s party. *D*, however, disagrees strongly with *A*'s decision, saying that *A* must go to *B*'s party, since *A* had already accepted that invitation.

Useful expressions

A	*D*
meet more people	the right thing to do
B won't even know	how would *you* feel

10 Controlling the conversation

In this unit, you will learn different ways that people control and change a conversation. You will study what to do to change the subject politely, how to show the other person that you are listening and understanding, and how to get the other person to repeat or speak more slowly when speaking with you.

Listen to the dialogues that follow, noting especially the ways in which one person pays attention, signals understanding, shows surprise, changes the subject, or gets the other person to repeat or talk more slowly.

1   DIALOGUES 🔊

Dialogue A

Larry: ... The Highgate Mall? Hmm ... Let me see ... You know where the McDonald's is on McKnight Road?
Mel: No...
Larry: Well, do you know where Ellsworth Lane is?
5 Mel: Sorry. I'm from out of town.
Larry: OK. Tell you what you do ... Go straight ahead here until you come to a big intersection. That's Swallow Run. There's a light there. Take a left at the light on Swallow Run, go about half a mile, and then there's a kind of Y in the road, so you
10 have to keep to the right. After that, take the first left you come to. That will be Ellsworth Lane, which takes you ...
Mel: I'm sorry, but I couldn't quite follow you. Could you explain it again a little slower, please? I'd appreciate it.
Larry: Sure. Sorry about that. Yeah, you take a left onto Swallow
15 Run. That's the first light here on this road.
Mel: OK.
Larry: And then about half a mile down the road there's a Y in the road, and you just keep to the right. Got that?
Mel: Keep to the right. Yeah.
20 Larry: Then after that, take the first left onto Ellsworth Lane.
Mel: Mm-hmm.

Larry: And Ellsworth will take you to McKnight Road. There's a
         light there. That's where the McDonald's is. You can't miss it.
Mel: OK.
25 Larry: So you turn right on McKnight and keep going and eventually
         you'll see the mall on your left. OK?
Mel: Yeah. And thanks a lot.
Larry: Well, good luck!
Mel: Thanks. Bye.
30 Larry: Bye.

mall: a shopping center with many stores under one roof

Discussion

1. What is the subject of this conversation?
2. What question has Mel just asked Larry when the dialogue begins?
3. Find the place where Mel interrupts Larry. Why does he do this?
4. Why does Larry apologize in line 14?
5. How does Mel show that he understands the directions Larry gave
   him? What expressions does he use?
6. What does Larry mean in line 23 when he says, "You can't miss
   it"?
7. Paraphrase Larry's expressions "Got that?" (in line 18) and
   "OK?" (in line 26), and Mel's "Mm-hmm" in line 21.
8. Where are the two speakers, do you think? How well do they
   know each other? What is the level of formality?

Dialogue B

Mrs. Jensen:	So you just came back from Phoenix. How was it?
Mrs. Whipple:	We had a wonderful time. The weather was beautiful.
Mrs. Jensen:	Oh, I'm glad.
Mrs. Whipple:	And we had the best vacation in years.
5 Mrs. Jensen:	Good for you. Did you see the Jacksons?
Mrs. Whipple:	I spoke with Doris on the phone, but we didn't get to see them.
Mrs. Jensen:	Oh, really? I'm surprised. You were such good friends before they left.
10 Mrs. Whipple:	Well, you know how it is. We have some great slides if you and George would like to come over some evening.
Mrs. Jensen:	Yes, we'd like that. But tell me, what *did* Doris Jackson have to say?
15 Mrs. Whipple:	Oh, well, just the usual. Oh, my goodness, look at the time – it's almost eleven o'clock. I'm afraid I have to go. I'll talk to you another time. Good-bye.
Mrs. Jensen:	Bye. (*to herself*) I wonder what happened between the Whipples and the Jacksons?

Discussion

1. How does Mrs. Jensen show she is listening? What expressions does she use?
2. In line 10, what is Mrs. Whipple doing? Why does she start talking about slides?
3. In lines 13–14, what is Mrs. Jensen trying to do?
4. In line 15, what does Mrs. Whipple do?
5. Why does Mrs. Jensen think something is wrong between the Whipples and the Jacksons?

2 CONTROLLING THE CONVERSATION

You have probably heard conversations where someone says things like this: "... yeah... uh-huh ... oh, really?... sure." These expressions help control the conversation or guide the discussion. There are expressions that show attention, understanding, or agreement; others that show surprise; some that change the subject of the conversation; and others that get the other person to repeat or slow down.

Showing attention, understanding, or agreement

Expressions such as "Yes" or "Mm-hmm" indicate to the other person that you are listening and that you want the speaker to continue to explain his or her ideas or opinions. Sometimes, these expressions (see Section 3) also show that you *agree* with the speaker. Their main function, however, is to show polite attention and to encourage the other person to continue talking.

Another important way of showing that you are listening is to use non-verbal behavior. For example, you usually look the speaker in the eye when listening, and this is a signal that you are paying attention. Nodding the head up and down shows attention, understanding, or agreement, or leaning forward in a chair shows that you are really interested in what is being said. This non-verbal behavior is usually combined with words, so that a person who is listening attentively will lean forward, nod, and say "Yes ... Mm-hmm..."

Showing surprise

Expressions such as "Really?," "No kidding," or "What?" indicate surprise, although they may also be used to show doubt or to disagree mildly with the other person (see Unit 9). Here again, non-verbal behavior is also used. To show surprise, people often open their eyes wide, lift their eyebrows, or even (in great surprise) open their mouth.

Changing the subject

In controlling the conversation, you may want to change the subject, perhaps because you are tired of it or because you feel uncomfortable talking about it.

Friend: ... and you should see the radio I got! It's got AM and FM, and four big speakers!

You: Well, that's very nice. Which reminds me, did you hear the results of the baseball game last night? The Pirates couldn't have lost again?!

Getting someone to repeat or slow down

It is normal for a person to misunderstand or not to hear the other person sometimes, so you should have no fear of asking someone to repeat or slow down. There are various ways of doing this, for instance: (direct) "Could you please repeat what you just said?" or (less direct) "I didn't catch what you just said." See Section 3 for more examples of this.

Discussion

What gestures do you use in your country to express surprise? agreement? attention? How do you change the subject of the conversation? Do you have rules about who may change the subject?

3 PHRASES 🔲

Directions: Listen to the following phrases on the tape as you read along here. Then practice saying them. The phrases near the top of the list are generally more formal than the ones near the bottom.

SHOWING ATTENTION, UNDERSTANDING, OR AGREEMENT

More formal
↕
Less formal

I see.
Exactly.
Yes.
Right.
Um-hmm.
Yeah.

SHOWING SURPRISE

Really?
Oh no!
No kidding!
What?
Oh my gosh!

CHANGING THE SUBJECT

Which reminds me...
Come to think of it,...
By the way,...

GETTING SOMEONE TO REPEAT OR SLOW DOWN

More formal
↕
Less formal

Would you mind repeating what you just said?
Could you please repeat that?
Would you say that again more slowly, please?
What did you say?
I didn't catch that.
Run that by me again.
What?

4 SMALL GROUP PRACTICE

A. Using what you've learned

Directions: For each situation that follows, read the cues given, then discuss the relationship among the speakers and the level of formality. Using this information, complete the dialogues orally with phrases from Section 3 or with any other appropriate response. Example:

A: ... Well, there was this woman who *talked all the time*.

B: Yeah?

A: *It was awful*.

B: Mm-hmm.

A: *She said outrageous things*.

B: Really?

Situation 1

A: ... and so I said to him, "Look, what difference does it make? I can always get a new job."

B:

C: Where were we on vacation? Oh, we were in Florida. Why?

B:

A:

Situation 2

A:

B: I'm sorry, but I didn't get that. _____?

A:

B: Oh, thanks.

Situation 3

A:

B: Well, I don't mean to change the subject, but _____.

A:

B:

Situation 4

A: I'm sorry, but I didn't get what you just said.

B:

A:

B. Cued dialogues

Directions: After looking at each situation carefully, discuss with your partner the relationship among the speakers and the appropriate level of formality. Then practice, using any words or expressions appropriate to express the functions given. Your teacher will ask you to perform the dialogue for the class.

Situation 1

Emma and Nels Jorgensen have just had a baby girl, so Nels is telling his friend Erik all about how the delivery went.

ERIK	NELS
1. greets Nels	1. returns greeting
2. asks what the news is	2. says it was a girl
3. congratulates Nels and Emma, asks how it went	3. tells what time Emma went to hospital
4. shows attention	4. tells how long he had to wait
5. shows surprise	5. describes how the baby looked
6. shows attention	6. gives the doctor's name
7. asks Nels to repeat	7. repeats doctor's name
8. shows attention, asks where Emma is now	8. gives information
9. promises to visit	9. expresses pleasure, thanks Erik
10. gives preclosing	10. replies to preclosing
11. says good-bye	11. says good-bye

Situation 2

A, the personal secretary of *B*, is sitting at work. *A* has a problem: *A* is writing a novel and has been taking a typewriter home at night to work on the book, even though *B* does not like that sort of thing. Today *A* has forgotten to bring the typewriter to the office and is hoping *B* will not notice that it is gone.

A	*B*
1. greets *B*	1. greets *A*, hands *A* a memo and asks *A* to type it immediately
2. changes subject by giving *B* urgent message	2. responds to message, asks *A* again to type the memo
3. offers to get *B* some fresh coffee	3. declines offer of coffee
4. compliments *B* on new suit	4. accepts compliment, gives information on suit
5. compliments *B*'s taste in clothes	5. responds to compliment, reminds *A* to type memo
6. agrees to type memo, gives preclosing	6. says good-bye
7. says good-bye	

C. Mini-roleplays

Directions: Discuss the situation with your partner and decide on the proper level of formality. You can use the suggested expressions if you want to. Then practice. When you are ready, perform for the class and discuss your performance with your teacher and classmates.

Roleplay 1

A, a sophomore in college, is spending the weekend at the house of a roommate's parents. This is *A*'s first visit, and *A* is trying to make a good impression by listening to one parent share childhood memories. It appears the parent had a very unusual childhood.

Useful expressions

A	THE PARENT
grow up around here?	10 brothers and sisters
hobbies as a child	all kinds of mischief
	large vegetable garden

Roleplay 2*

Student A

You wish to buy a car. You are in a used-car dealer's and you see a second-hand car that might be suitable. You decide to find out more about it, for example, how old it is, who the previous owner was, how expensive it is to run, how many miles it gets to the gallon, and whether there is a warranty. You have about $2,000 cash.

Student B

You are a used-car salesperson. You see a customer looking at a car on the lot. The car is 2 years old and belonged previously to the leader of a local rock group. It gets about 15 miles to the gallon. There was a new transmission put in 3 months ago. Your company offers a 3-month warranty. You can arrange a car loan through a local bank. You are asking $3,110 for the car, although you can negotiate.

Roleplay 3

A is working as a waitress in a restaurant. One of the customers, B, needs to know how to drive from the restaurant to a certain hotel in the center of town. After paying the bill, B asks A for help. A explains, but has to repeat the directions, because they are a little complicated.

Useful expressions

A	B
right at the first light	directions to the Starlight?
left at the third light	I'm not from this part of town
post office on the (left)	
keep going until you see...	

---

*Adapted from William Littlewood, *Communicative Language Teaching* (Cambridge University Press, 1981), pp. 55–6.

11 Getting information

Every day we are confronted with situations that require us to obtain information from strangers. We need to find out where an unfamiliar street or office is, for example, or we need more information on plane schedules or car prices before we can make a decision.

As you listen to the dialogues that follow, listen for the ways in which the speakers obtain information from others, and the ways in which one person gives information to the other.

1 DIALOGUES

Dialogue A

(The telephone rings.)
Box Office: Warner Theater.
Jennifer: Yes, what are you showing this week?
Box Office: Well, starting today we have *Cold Feet* and *The Lost Soul*.
Jennifer: *Cold Feet and the Lost Soul*? I've never heard of that movie. Who's in it?
5 Box Office: I'm sorry, but you misunderstood. Those are two movies. *Cold Feet* is the first one, and then *The Lost Soul* is after that.

Jennifer: Oh, I didn't realize it was a double feature.
Box Office: Yes, we always have a double feature during the week.
10 Jennifer: Could you tell me when the first one starts?
Box Office: Seven-fifteen.
Jennifer: OK, thanks a lot. Bye.
Box Office: You're welcome. Bye.

double feature: two movies shown in sequence, for the price of one

Discussion

1. What is a "box office"?
2. Who are the two speakers? Do they know each other?
3. Why did Jennifer call the box office?
4. What words does Jennifer use to ask for information?
5. What is the misunderstanding about?
6. Paraphrase line 1.
7. What words show that this is a polite conversation?

Dialogue B

Frank Keaton: Excuse me, ma'am. Could you tell me how to get to
                    Carnegie Library from here?
Mrs. McAllister: Of course. It's on Tenth Street, just across from the
                    Armory.
5   Frank: On Tenth?
Mrs. McAllister: That's right. You know where that is?
Frank: I'm afraid I don't. I'm new in town.
Mrs. McAllister: Well, do you know where the old Post Office is?
Frank: No, I don't. But I do know where Sears is.
10 Mrs. McAllister: I'm not sure that's going to help us. Let me see...
                    Why don't you follow this street, Paddington Way,
                    until you get to the stoplight. Take a right there,
                    that's Elm Street, and go up about two or three
                    blocks, until you get to Tenth. Then turn left. The
15   library is on your right about three blocks down.
Frank: Let me get this straight... Go up to Elm, take a
                    right, go three blocks...
Mrs. McAllister: That's right, two or three.
Frank: ... turn left on Tenth, and the library is on the
20   right-hand side, three blocks down.
Mrs. McAllister: That's right.
Frank: Well, thank you very much, ma'am. You've been
                    very helpful!
Mrs. McAllister: That's quite all right.

Usage note: "Ma'am" is often used in the southern United States. It is
a polite way of addressing women.

Unit 11

Discussion

1. Identify the two speakers in this dialogue. Where are they?
2. What does Frank need? How does he get Mrs. McAllister's attention?
3. What words does Frank use to obtain the necessary information?
4. Paraphrase line 5.
5. What function is Mrs. McAllister performing in lines 10–15?
6. Why does Frank repeat the directions?
7. Give some examples that show that this is a rather formal conversation. What accounts for that formality?

2   GETTING INFORMATION

In most cases, if you need information, you can ask someone directly. However, there are some topics considered personal and private that Americans are hesitant to discuss. These include salary, age, weight, and political or religious beliefs, or the cost of particular items. On the other hand, many Americans are quite free with information about their children, their health, their friends and neighbors. Once again, these customs vary according to regional differences. You can "soften" direct questions by asking indirect questions to show an interest and to gain information.

Instead of: How much do you make a year?   *Use this*: About how much does a secretary (or an engineer) make?

Instead of: How much was that rug?   *Use this*: What are they getting for oriental rugs these days?

Calling on the telephone

You can get information over the phone about hours of operation, availability and cost of items, and public services. A good source of written information is the local phone book and the Yellow Pages.

When requesting information over the phone, state exactly what you want. Notice that in Dialogue A, the caller thanks the person for the information. Sometimes the preclosing is omitted in these calls.

If you call a department store or a company with many offices, your call will be answered by a switchboard operator. The operator will answer by saying the name of the company. Tell him or her what you want. Then you will be put on "hold" while the operator finds the person you want. When you are on hold, the line is usually silent; you just wait until the person comes on to talk to you.

Operator: Kaufmann's.
You: I'd like the furniture department, please.
Operator: Hold, please. (*click*)
Clerk: Furniture, Tom Jones speaking.
You: Yes, do you have...

Asking someone on the street

On the street people often ask strangers for directions; for information about public transportation, buses, and taxis; and for the time. A
crowded bus stop is a good place to ask for directions, because someone is likely to know and the rules for overhearing a conversation
apply (see Unit 8).

You: Can you tell me how to get to South Side Hospital?
Stranger: Go two blocks down (*gestures*) and turn right. You
can't miss it.
You: Thanks.

You: Do all the buses go downtown?
Stranger 1: I don't know. I'm new here. Sorry.
Stranger 2: All the ones with a red sticker in the window go
downtown.
You: Thanks.

Stranger: Do you have the time?
You: (*looking at your watch*) Three-fifteen.
Stranger: Thanks.

or

Stranger: Do you have the time?
You: (*holding up your empty wrist*) Sorry.
Stranger: Thanks anyway.

In a store

If you're in a large store, you may want to know where a specific department is. To ask a clerk, first get his or her attention, if necessary, and ask:

You: Excuse me, Miss. Where's the children's department?
Clerk: Third floor, to the right of the escalator.
You: Thanks.
Clerk: Sure.

Discussion

What formalities do you have for using the telephone? Are there certain ritual greetings? partings? Are there certain "taboo" subjects in asking questions? Can you ask someone, for instance, what his or her salary is, or how much money they paid for a certain item?

---

3 PHRASES 🔲

Directions: Listen to the following phrases on the tape as you read along here. Then practice saying them. The phrases near the top of the list are generally more formal than the ones near the bottom.

ON THE TELEPHONE

Could you please tell me your hours?
Can you please tell me when you close?

FACE-TO-FACE

More	Excuse me. Could you (please) tell me the way to...?
formal	Pardon me. Could you please tell me how to get to...?
↑	Could you tell me where (the nearest restroom) is? (*Note the inverted word order.*)
│	Can you tell me where (the library) is?
↓	(Excuse me.) How do I get to...?
Less	Is this the way to...?
formal	Do you know where (the post office) is?

Remember: The person getting the information always says "Thank you," and the giver usually says some version of "You're welcome" (see Unit 4).

4 SMALL GROUP PRACTICE

A. Using what you've learned

Directions: For each situation that follows, read the cues given, then discuss the relationship among the speakers and the level of formality. Using this information, complete the dialogues orally with phrases from Section 3 or any other appropriate response. Example:

A: Good morning. May I help you?

B: *I'd like a room for two, please.*

A: What kind of room would you like?

B: *One on the beach side.*

A: *How long will you be with us?*

B: We plan to be here just two nights.

A: *How about a double on the front?*

B: That will be fine.

A: *Good. Sign here, please.*

Situation 1

A:
B: You mean St. Luke's Hospital?
A:
B: That's easy. Just...
A:
B: Don't mention it.

Situation 2

A: Good afternoon. Reed Hardware.
B:
A: We're open from... to...
B: What about Saturdays?
A:
B:
A: You're welcome.

Situation 3

A:

B: Do you know where Main Street is? Well, it's on the corner of Fourth and Main.

A:

B: Fourth is just a block over from Fifth, right? You know where that is, don't you?

A:

B:

A: OK. I think I've got it now. Thanks a lot.

B:

B. Cued dialogues

Directions: After looking at each situation carefully, discuss with your partner the relationship among the speakers and the appropriate level of formality. Then practice, using any words or expressions appropriate to express the functions given. Your teacher will ask you to perform the dialogue for the class.

Situation 1

A is new in the country and is trying to find the consulate. *A* sees a police officer across the street.

A	*POLICE OFFICER*
1. gets police officer's attention	1. responds
2. explains situation, asks where consulate is	2. gives directions
3. asks for clarification	3. explains again
4. repeats directions	4. confirms directions
5. thanks police officer	5. replies to thanks

Situation 2

A calls the airport to make reservations to fly home to see his or her parents for two weeks. A wants to fly on Friday, but doesn't know when the planes leave or how much the round trip will cost.

A	AIRLINE REPRESENTATIVE
	1. answers phone (_____ Airlines)
2. states need for information on flights	2. offers to help with information
3. asks for scheduled departures on Friday	3. gives times of departure
4. asks for fare information	4. asks whether it is round-trip or one-way
5. answers the question	5. gives the fare, offers to make a reservation
6. makes a reservation or declines offer to make a reservation	6. thanks customer for calling
7. gives closing	7. replies to closing

Situation 3

A wants to call a friend in West Germany, but may not have enough money to pay for it. A calls Information to ask about types of calls and rates.

A	OPERATOR (INFORMATION)
	1. answers call
2. describes type of call wanted	2. identifies it as a station-to-station call
3. asks for rates	3. gives rates (per minute)
4. asks for cheapest time to call	4. gives information
5. thanks Operator	5. replies to thanks

C. Mini-roleplays

Directions: Discuss the situation with your partner(s) and decide on the proper level of formality. You can use the suggested expressions if you want to. Then practice. When you are ready, perform for the class and discuss your performance with your teacher and classmates.

Roleplay 1

A and B, two good friends from the university, are in Miami for a conference. After checking on hotel prices, they have decided to share a room for the week, to save some money. Now they are about to check in at the Sheraton Hotel.

Useful expressions

FRONT DESK CLERK	*A*	*B*
May I help you?	staying six nights	room for two
double rooms	twin beds	how much?
13th floor	use my Visa charge	room with a view
name?		
to register fill out this card		

Roleplay 2

A has an interview for a job as a dental technician. Dr. B is interviewing A for the job. (Remember to use opening and closing formulas.)

Useful expressions

B	*A*
make yourself comfortable	appreciate your seeing me
your background in medicine	medical school 2 years
graduate school	two-year technical program
any experience?	summer work for Dr. Peters
when available?	

Roleplay 3

Divide the class into pairs. Read the general situation information. X's version is on page 114 and Y's version is on page 113. They should then discuss this together.

Then X and Y should each read the specific information that follows the general information. They should *not* share this information, but use it to arrange the meeting.

Agent Y

General situation: You and your partner are undercover agents working for an international agency that is trying to promote world peace. You have to fly to Seattle to pick up an envelope containing some top secret information that your organization needs immediately.

You call your partner, Agent X, to arrange your flight from Chicago to Seattle, and your return to Chicago the same day. You must find the quickest return possible, for it is very dangerous for you to be seen in Seattle.

Your goal in this phone call is to arrange the time and place of meeting, and to decide how you will get the envelope from Agent X.

You have never seen Agent X before.

Your specific information: It takes about 6 minutes to change gates at the airport. It will take you one minute to meet Agent X and obtain the envelope.

DAILY FLIGHT SCHEDULE – NORTHWEST ORIENT
(all times are local)

DEPARTS CHICAGO/O'HARE	ARRIVES SEATTLE/TACOMA	
7:05 a.m.	7:15 a.m.	non-stop
12:45 p.m.	2:35 p.m.	2 stops
4:50 p.m.	5:30 p.m.	1 stop
9:35 p.m.	9:45 p.m.	non-stop

You arrive at Gate 7, on the Blue Concourse.

Agent X

General situation: You and your partner are undercover agents working for an international agency that is trying to promote world peace. You have an envelope of top secret information that your partner, Agent Y, is going to pick up from you at the Seattle/Tacoma airport. Agent Y will be flying in from Chicago. Your organization in Chicago needs this secret information immediately.

Agent Y is supposed to call you to make arrangements with you to pick up the envelope. You have some scheduling information that Y will need.

Since Agent Y is known in Seattle, it is very dangerous for Y to be there very long. Y must make the return flight as soon as possible after landing.

Your goal in this conversation will be to give Agent Y the information needed to make travel plans and to arrange the time and place of your meeting. You have never met before.

Your specific information: You have a map of the airport (page 115). Agent Y does not.

DAILY FLIGHT SCHEDULE – NORTHWEST ORIENT
(all times are local)

DEPARTS SEATTLE/TACOMA	ARRIVES CHICAGO/O'HARE	
7:25 a.m.	11:30 a.m.	non-stop
3:05 p.m.	7:10 p.m.	non-stop
5:45 p.m.	10:45 p.m.	2 stops
10:00 p.m.	2:05 a.m.	non-stop

All flights depart from Gate 30, on the Green Concourse.

You know that the airport security check will take 3 minutes to get through, since there may be a line. You also know that check-in and seating at Gate 30 will take at least 5 minutes.

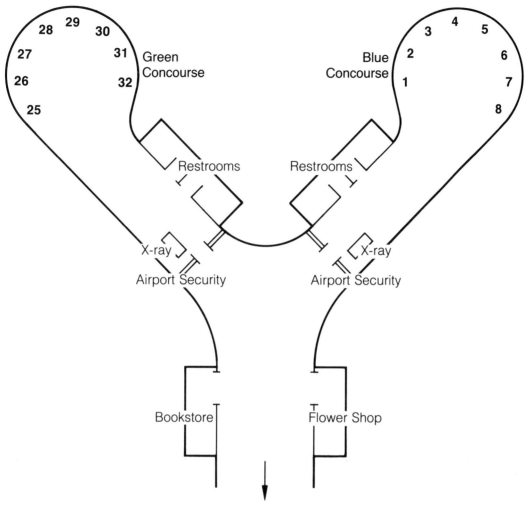

Seattle/Tacoma airport: Agent X's map.